Resistant Students

Reach Me Before You Teach Me

Mary Skvorak

ROWMAN & LITTLEFIELD EDUCATION
A division of
ROWMAN & LITTLEFIELD PUBLISHERS, INC.
Lanham • New York • Toronto • Plymouth, UK

Published by Rowman & Littlefield Education
A division of Rowman & Littlefield Publishers, Inc.
A wholly owned subsidary of The Rowman & Littlefield Publishing Group, Inc.
4501 Forbes Boulevard, Suite 200, Lanham, Maryland 20706
www.rowman.com

10 Thornbury Road, Plymouth PL6 7PP, United Kingdom

British Library Cataloguing in Publication Information Available

Library of Congress Cataloging-in-Publication Data

Skvorak, Mary, 1940– .
Resistant students : reach me before you teach me / Mary Skvorak.
p. cm.
Includes bibliographical references.
ISBN 978-1-61048-908-9 (cloth : alk. paper) — ISBN 978-1-61048-909-6 (pbk. : alk. paper) —
ISBN 978-1-61048-910-2 (ebook) (print)
1. Problem children—Education. 2. Motivation in education. I. Title.
LC4801.S56 2012
371.93—dc23
2012032264

☉™ The paper used in this publication meets the minimum requirements of American
National Standard for Information Sciences Permanence of Paper for Printed Library
Materials, ANSI/NISO Z39.48-1992.

Printed in the United States of America

Dedicated to the elementary school, middle school, high school and
college students who were my teachers.

Contents

Preface

I still love teaching. It has been my great good fortune to be a teacher for most of five decades. Fifty-five expectant fifth-grade faces greeted me in the fall of 1961, happily unaware of my inexperience.

By 1989, I was able to say that I taught children in schools that represented every socioeconomic background. I spent the majority of those years with middle-school students. Teaching students in the inner city brought me the highest level of job satisfaction. I decided to return there to complete my school teaching career.

As a "teacher on special assignment," I became part of a program designed to reduce the high rate of recidivism among students returning to regular classrooms after having been on long-term suspension for serious behavioral issues. My job was to offer as much one-to-one support as possible to those students to help them stay in school. Interacting with their teachers, parents, guardians, social workers, and parole officers gave me an unusual insight into the life experiences of this student group.

For these students, resisting the personal challenge and pitfalls that learning represented seemed an inevitable outcome. The situations and circumstances of their life outside of school sapped their energy, still leaving mountains of social and emotional issues unattended. The more positive and personal the connection I made, the more successful my attempts became to draw them into believing they could learn.

In 1988, I also welcomed the chance to teach evening classes in the School of Education at Nazareth College of Rochester. The education textbook theories, strategies, and teaching techniques we studied by night were tested and tried in my classroom by day. I taught at least one education course at Nazareth every semester for twenty-one years. Eventually, it was my privilege to direct the Undergraduate Inclusive Elementary Education Program for seven years.

And so it is that my fifth-grade students, and the students after them, provided me with the experiences that made it possible for every example in this book to be true. Neither they nor I would ever have guessed that they would teach me as much, if not more, than I ever taught them.

I offer my sincerest thanks to Marilyn Draxl, Nancy Niemi, Kathy Russell, and David Skvorak, who were readers of my manuscript-in-progress. They offered insights, corrections, directions, and advice generously and kindly. Because of them, this book is better than it would otherwise have been.

M. S.

Introduction

Behavior management will be a timely topic as long as there is schooling. Every teacher knows that academic instruction is not delivered in a vacuum, but to unique individuals whose life experiences, ability, and personality affect the learning process. Successful teaching requires skillful teachers who have the knowledge and the dispositions that demonstrate their understanding of both the cognitive and affective needs of children.

Numerous excellent books about behavior management agree that building relationships with students is imperative. Teachers maximize learning when students feel personally encouraged, valued, and rewarded for their efforts. Few books offer specific examples that show how creating positive personal connections look in actual classroom situations. This book offers concrete examples from authentic practice derived from established theories of education.

Each chapter is a building block that guides the reader from basic information about forming relationships to more complex material and refined possibilities for how to establish positive personal connections with students, especially those who are resistant learners. Examples feature teacher-student dialogue to capture situations and exchanges that do not yield positive results. Those situations and exchanges are compared with reframed teacher-student dialogue that holds promise for building bridges that lead to relationships and improved academic achievement.

Chapter 1 explains how the foundation for secure relationships rests in having had the good fortune to form healthy attachments with parents or caregivers. It follows that positive and negative self-talk emerges from life experiences and impacts interactions that relate to relationships with others. That is why chapter 2 also points out how important it is for teachers to recognize the power and influence their own self-talk wields in situations

that require unemotional responses. Chapter 3 addresses the inevitable conflict that occurs in daily classroom life. It invites those who wish to make
positive personal connections with students to view conflict as an opportunity to change unproductive behaviors.

Because many unproductive behaviors are rooted in anger, chapter 4 ex-
amines how to manage anger in the classroom and ways to help students
begin to attempt self-management. The next chapter investigates how the use
of punishment contraindicates motivation and arrests trust, a prerequisite for
relationships. Chapter 6 concentrates on how to increase motivation by rein-
forcing desired behaviors effectively without the use of rewards that are
bribes. The value and joy of receiving a reward that is not a bribe unlocks
many closed doors and can open veritable floodgates for kindness, care,
compassion, and happiness. Having a "new" mind-set about using rewards
connects to recognizing that every student has gifts, talents, special interests,
or ways of thinking that can serve as reasons to create positive personal
connections. This is the theme in chapter 7.

Lastly, the reader is invited to explore avenues not traveled often
enough—self-examination, leaving one's comfort zone, and testing one's
resolve to make a difference when the challenge to do so is great. The end of
every chapter offers summary Points to Remember as suggestions for action,
intending to complement the choices readers may select for their own personal use.

The plentiful examples in this book, hopefully, will prompt the reader to
feel empowered enough to belie the phrase, "when all is said and done, more
is always said than done."

Chapter 1

If Houses Are Built upon Sand . . .

No such thing as teachers who care. Don't need 'em anyway. I take care of
myself.
—*Tierra, age twelve*

Look—I've given you as many chances as I'm going to. If you don't want to
learn what I'm teaching, that's fine. I get paid anyway.
—*Mr. Diamond, seventh-grade social studies teacher*

Relationships matter. Research shows the value and importance of positive
student/teacher relationships at all grade levels. Teachers debate what the
depth and degree of their relationship with students ought to be, but none
would deny that it is better to have a good relationship with students than not
to have one:[1]

- Successful classroom management depends on it.
- Academic achievement enhances it.
- Students' self-esteem develops better because of it.
- Teachers' job satisfaction influences it.

What skills must teachers learn, what dispositions must they have in order to
enjoy the benefits of positive teacher/student relationships? Is it possible to
form relationships with students who seem steadfastly unwilling to do so?
Teachers with insight who make forming relationships with all of their students a priority and who can draw from a reserve of strong interpersonal
skills become the memorable ones. They truly make a difference in children's lives.

FOUNDATIONS FOR SECURE RELATIONSHIPS

Human relationships are complex. They have their roots in attachments formed in infancy. Children struggle to develop loving relationships with others if they do not bond or form healthy attachment to their parents or primary caregivers when they are very young.[2] Contributing reasons for poor or faulty attachments among children are well-known problems in our present society. Some are: marital discord; genetic influences; post-partum depression; physical, sexual, and psychological abuse or neglect; overly harsh or inconsistent discipline; teenage pregnancies; too-late adoptions; poor day care; poverty; and social disadvantage.

For these reasons and others, there will always be children in schools everywhere whose parents or primary caregivers have neither the skills nor the resources to meet their children's basic physical, cognitive, social, and moral development needs. These children depend on others to rescue them from the dire consequences of their unearned circumstances. Teachers have the good fortune to stand in loco parentis by virtue of their profession. They can and do meet the developmental needs of children during the school day.

Healthy attachment leads to the development of trust in others and self-reliance, whereas unattached children battle feelings of anger or even rage, have poor impulse control, and have difficulty learning basic social and cognitive skills.[3]

In school, many children who experience poor attachment with their primary caregivers are the ones most resistant to forming relationships with teachers or peers. They appear to have built impenetrable walls around their feelings. Unfortunately, their protection is also their prison. This type of child offers teachers an invitation par excellence to be the one, perhaps the *first* one, to offer hope, optimism about life, social skill development, and a personal experience of warmth and caring at school.

Teachers who can accept this invitation will already be persons who are capable of empathy. Their life experiences may give them insight into the perspective of the students whom they teach. It may not. For some teachers, even the easier motivation to help someone who has a similar background, culture, or other commonality is frequently absent. Some teachers' professional training contributes to their ability to recognize the impact harsh life experience has had on some children and enables them to call upon affective skills to care for children in obvious need.

Forming positive personal connections with challenging youngsters such as these is neither a small nor an insignificant task. Teachers who do it successfully as a matter of habit are models of genuine altruism brought to practical application by acquired skills in understanding human behavior.

Troubled children are easily recognized. Any teacher can quickly label them as angry, antisocial, disobedient, annoying, spoiled, unfriendly, defiant, irritable, or hostile. Can children be "damaged beyond repair," destined to become troubled adults, despite genuine interventions? Yes. However, *most* children in school are not at the farthest end of the continuum that represents complete attachment failure.

Many children only need to experience warm, consistent, stable relationships with adults. Teachers are often the ones in the very best position to offer such support, because so many hours are spent in school. Students who value their teachers' opinions and trust that their attention is sincere will show measurable academic achievement and social growth.

In their collaborative studies of at-risk youth, Larry Bredtro, Steve Von Bockern, and Martin Brokenleg ask teachers to note:[4]

> Practice and young people themselves confirm that the attention and concern of caring and careful individuals, at specific times, can mean the world—literally and figuratively, to children who are struggling to hold on to hope and to develop a sense of themselves as valued and valuable human beings.

By nature, human beings have a deep need to belong. Movies, songs, and poetry celebrate the value of belonging. In the movie *It's a Wonderful Life*, every viewer loves the scene where the townsfolk gather to publicly say how each has been touched by Jimmy Stewart's character, George Bailey. Songs say people who need people are lucky. Poets speak eloquently about our connection to the universe. Agreement is universal when the media use the maxim, "It takes a village to raise a child."

The nuclear family is no longer the norm. Families of all types assert that feeling isolated and lonely are common outcomes of the mobile society that puts so much distance between friends and other family members. "Bedroom" communities and "latchkey" children are familiar terms. Many schools are large, creating bureaucracies that make personal service between and among teachers, students, parents, and support staff difficult and burdensome.

Understanding attachment formation and the need children have to belong are the bedrock upon which teachers can build relationships with students for learning and for life, perhaps even with those who seem most unwilling, defiant, and oppositional.

POSITIVE AND NEGATIVE ASPECTS OF RESISTANCE

"Resistance" is a word whose first connotation is frequently negative. Its meaning, "to strive to fend off or offset the actions, effects or force of someone or something," can elicit strong emotional responses.[5] Often it brings us memories of conflict and power struggles, maybe even fear.

In school, resistance is no stranger at teachers' door of daily experience. When students' classroom behavior presents itself as hostile, disrespectful, uncooperative, self-centered, immature, lazy, violent, or very passive, the gauntlet is thrown. Teachers have no choice but to deal with students' misbehavior one way or another.

Particularly challenging are students disconnected from the learning process and unresponsive to ordinary interventions. *How* teachers deal with students' misbehavior is the essential question. Their answer determines in large part whether school will reinforce the weak attachment cycle of these children and contribute to their further alienation or be a place that interrupts that cycle.

Gene Maeroff identifies social capital as experiencing stability in a caring environment and having trusting relationships. As children grow, Maeroff suggests, their support systems should engender a sense of well-being, connectedness with others, academic initiative and a sense of knowing. Like money in the bank, they should be able to draw from a wealth of positive life experiences that offset whatever daily challenges they encounter at school or at home.[6]

In school, teachers easily recognize students who lack social capital. Their empty experience bank may represent many causes, but all have nearly the same effect—a need for extra support. For teachers to contribute social capital to students, especially to those most in need, two conscious choices are necessary:

1. Recognize that students' resistance has powerful and positive aspects.
2. Actively develop the ability to reframe negative situations into positive opportunities.

What's good about resistance? For some children, resistance is protection. It provides a place free from risk of further emotional hurt and allows respite from feelings too intense to process. Powerless children often find significant relief when they are able to control their parents, teachers, or other adults in authority through passivity or aggression. People such as Mahatma Gandhi, Martin Luther King Jr., Rosa Parks, Mother Teresa, and Anne Frank have shown how resistance draws strength from altruism and a strong moral sense.

Teachers who recognize the positive aspects of resistance can begin to help students discover protection, relief, and strength by building trusting relationships with them. The support that a positive relationship offers enables students to find courage to begin to leave behind their dark fears about people, places, and things and walk toward a brighter, healthier future.

Students who resist learning quickly are labeled as failures. Herbert Kohl makes a compelling distinction between failure and not learning. He says about not learning: "It tends to strengthen the will, clarify one's definition of self, reinforce self-discipline and provide inner satisfaction."[7]

Some students might elect not to learn because they feel doing so means denying cultural beliefs unappreciated in the school setting in which they find themselves. Some students may choose not to learn because they feel their teacher does not fairly represent more than one side of any issue. Some students are not ready to yield any trust in what an adult says or does.

Without question, we draw our life's meaning from experiences and interactions with myriad social forces. The time in which we live, our race, culture, socioeconomic position, gender, parents, relatives, neighbors, education opportunities, and religious beliefs shape our perception and judgments daily.

Social psychology tells us that our *thoughts* quickly accompany *feelings* that can and often do translate into *actions*. This is not to say that our perception and judgments are accurate. They often are not. Learning to reframe *first* thoughts, *first* feelings, and, especially, *first* actions is an essential skill for professional educators.

Strong emotions, for example, upset the *thought/feeling/action* balance and can cause teacher and/or student behavior to be irrational. For this reason, teachers who actively develop the ability to reframe negative situations into positive opportunities use objective judgment in situations instead of subjective judgment. They recognize the influence their personal biases and worldview have on their feelings and daily interactions with students.

FIVE WAYS TO REFRAME NEGATIVE SITUATIONS INTO POSITIVE OPPORTUNITIES

In difficult student-teacher encounters, typically the first action is rooted in an emotion-driven first thought and first feeling. Knowledge, skill, and intentional practice can easily reframe such first thoughts and feelings.

Second thoughts, second feelings, and second actions are more insightful and productive. The teacher's aim is deliberate—to model an alternative adult response to that which is anticipated. Reframing first thoughts and feelings is often the first step toward establishing a positive personal connection with a student that could lead to building a relationship.

Five examples follow of typical teacher-student encounters, with suggestions and dialogue about how to reframe each one:

Example #1

Teachers who successfully form relationships with their students resist imme-diate judgment when their students' inappropriate behavior elicits an emo-tional response.

Typical Encounter:

> Abe: *"I will NOT take off my hat! Get out of my face!"*

The student who displays this behavior expects the receiver of such inflam-matory disrespect to react in a predictable, hostile way. A teacher's first internal response will likely be to fulfill the student's expectation and cast an internal negative judgment about the student. This is understandable. But, it is a response fed by emotion.

> Ms. Williams's first thought: *"I don't EVER have to take such disrespect from a child, troubled or not!"*

An internal negative judgment (thought) comes immediately, unbidden, drawn from long established inner speech and personal values.

> Ms. Williams's first feeling: *Anger, impatience, hurt, insult, embarrass-ment. Concomitant feelings register, connected to the thought.*

> Ms. Williams's first action: *Student WILL remove hat and/or face punish-ing consequence. Action uses rightful authority to force student submis-sion.*

Reframed Encounter:

> Abe: *"I will NOT take off my hat! Get out of my face!"*

Ms. Williams's first thought and first feeling will be the same, *except that she will not allow emotion to drive her action.*

> Ms. Williams's second thought: *"Here's a young man with serious is-sues. I wonder what's behind all this bravado? I'm going to avoid this power struggle right now."*

Second internal thought sets aside initial judgment.

> Ms. Williams's second feeling: *Concern, curiosity, challenge.*

More rational, empathic feelings follow second thought and compete with those first registered.

> Ms. Williams's second action: *Response that reaches out without hostility.*

> Ms. Williams: "Well, Abe. I can see that I'm not going to get you to take off your hat. I'm surprised you're so angry with me for asking. I'm sorry such a small thing has upset you."

Action does not use rightful authority; instead, it fails to support student's expectation.

This response reveals a great deal about Ms. Williams's ability to change a negative situation into a positive opportunity.

- Did the teacher recognize the need to respond differently from the student's expectations? Yes. An unexpected response like this will challenge the student's stereotype about teachers' use of authority.
- Did the teacher recognize that her first response was rooted in emotion rather than reason? Yes.
- Did the teacher display respect toward a student who did not "deserve" it at the moment? Yes. Again, the student's expectation is met quite differently.
- Did the teacher's response show realization that the student's attack was not personal? Yes.
- Did the teacher have to make a judgment that the power struggle avoided was worth the chance for future dialogue with this difficult student? Yes.

Remember, relationships with students cannot emerge from power struggles because the authoritative action that wins the contest reinforces the student's false perception that teachers are not allies. In effect, battles lose the war when the cause is less important than the outcome.

Example #2

Teachers who successfully form relationships with their students can differentiate between labeling a student and labeling a student's behavior.

The chronically unprepared student is frequently labeled lazy. That may be true, but attributing "lazy" to the student instead of to the student's behavior sets a negative thought/feeling/action pattern. Deciding to investigate the cause of his behavior, especially if his unpreparedness accompanies hostility, requires an extraordinary teacher.

Typical Encounter:

> Susan: *"No. I didn't do the packet. No. I don't have a book. No. I didn't bring a pencil."*
>
> Mr. Luria's first thought: *"Susan is just plain lazy. I know a lazy girl when I see one."*
>
> Mr. Luria's first feeling: *Frustration, discouragement, ineffectiveness*
>
> Mr. Luria's first action: *Ignore Susan. Can't change lazy.*

The decision to act this way makes forming a connection with this student impossible. It makes forming a relationship very unlikely.

Reframed Encounter:

> Susan: *"No. I didn't do the packet. No. I don't have a book. No. I didn't bring a pencil."*

Most students who are chronically unprepared demonstrate a need beyond the easy "lazy" label. In a busy classroom, they offer busy teachers unbelievable frustration on every level.

> Mr. Luria's second thought: *"Susan seems to be plain lazy. Poor girl. I wonder if that's it or if there is something else behind her behavior."*
>
> Mr. Luria's second feeling: *Sympathy, hopefulness, readiness to help her.*
>
> Mr. Luria's second action: *Probe more into why Susan is chronically unprepared.*
>
> Mr. Luria, sincerely: *"Susan, I'm sorry that you're not prepared for today. Here's a pencil, at least. Listen, I have a great idea about something good! (Smiling): Would you please meet with me for just a few minutes during X? (lunch? after school? in the hallway?) I want to see what you think of my idea."* (The "idea" only need be a chance to make a positive personal connection with Susan to speak informally about things that help some students get their work done, etc.)

The prospect of forming a connection between this teacher and student has changed from impossible to likely. Why?

- The teacher's response was different from the student's expectations.

- The teacher separated Susan's extrinsic behavior from her intrinsic value as a child.
- Susan can entertain the possibility that her teacher likes her.
- The teacher's willingness to meet with Susan indicates an openness that underpins all beginning relationships.

Example #3

Teachers who successfully form relationships with students can recast a negative trait into a positive prospect.

Disobedient students cause the ship to rock and roll, bring extra work to administrators and send teachers into the endless labyrinth of punishing consequences. Sometimes, for the sake of order, it is necessary to act upon immediate solutions for slight or serious disobedience. A teacher may choose to honor a negative thought/feeling/action set—for example, "My rule is NO gum!"/"I will be obeyed!"/"Throw it out!"

Other incidents may require quick and necessary use of authority. For example, egregious public disrespect, threats to the safety of the class, violent actions, or serious threats of violence call for immediate and strong use of authority without equivocation. Apart from such incidents, students who habitually display resistance to authority may really be inviting a teacher to take an interest in them.

The students who choose to confront teachers or classmates in public defiance of school rules have not learned that they may have qualities such as independent thinking, conviction, and/or leadership that have the potential to become personality strengths instead of weaknesses. Reframing students' liability—strong will, egotism, passive aggression—whichever it may be, into its positive asset could be key to making a positive personal connection. Students are often surprised to hear that their liabilities can be assets. That discovery can lead them to self-motivated change.

Typical Encounter:

Dante: *"Well, I LIKE doing things my own way. Most of these school rules are stupid, anyhow. I don't care what you say."*

Mrs. Caranova's first thought: *"Here we go again. The world according to Dante. He's offering his sassy opinion to the wrong person!"*

Mrs. Caranova's first feeling: *impatience, annoyance, disdain.*

Mrs. Caranova's first action: *Defend "rules"; make Dante comply; encourage his alienation from the group.*

Reframed Encounter:

> Dante: *"Well, I LIKE doing things my own way. Most of these school rules are stupid, anyhow. I don't care what you say."*

More often than not, students who say, "I don't care," are saying they have no hope.

> Mrs. Caranova's second thought: *"Here we go again. The world according to Dante. I wonder if that boy could ever be helped to control his mouth or anything else. Should I even try?"*

Whether or not to try is an important question when teachers consider using the second thought process. Building a relationship with a student who demonstrates at-risk school and/or personal behaviors will require *ongoing and consistent effort* on the part of intervening teachers before the student trusts that their behavior is reliably different from his or her former expectation.

Teachers should expect a rocky road. Usually, students will ameliorate their behavior for a while. Then they will test the adult to see if the unexpected response is reliable in a different situation. If the student decides the adult response is predictable and trustworthy, the relationship will begin in earnest. To abandon a relationship once begun will reinforce the negative stereotypes about adults as helpers even more.

> Mrs. Caranova's second feeling: *Sensitivity to Dante's need for intervention, acceptance of Dante as he is right now, optimism*

> Mrs. Caranova's second action: *Patient attempt to interact with Dante.*

> Mrs. Caranova: *"You know, Dante, when I was your age I never would have had the nerve to speak my mind the way you do. Learning to do that respectfully would make you quite powerful. Really! It is true that rules sometimes don't do what they're supposed to do, and it's good that you can see that. Wow. I can see so many qualities in you that make you a strong person. For now . . ."* (Mrs. Caranova might or might not have to enforce the rule.)

Mrs. Caranova may or may not meet with Dante personally and privately to address how his habitually offensive self-expression is a liability instead of an asset. Still, a seed for relationship has been planted because:

- The teacher's response to Dante's rationale for being exempt from school rules is different from Dante's expectations.

- The teacher's unexpected and specific praise for Dante will, at least internally, get Dante's attention and likely soften his attitude toward this teacher.
- The teacher has created a positive set that will allow further interaction that can be pursued even when a punishment for disobedience, such as an after-school or lunch detention, brings Dante to this teacher's attention again.

Example #4

Teachers who successfully form relationships with their students recognize how their own weaknesses personify some of their students' actions.

It is common for us to be critical of people whose behavior is a reflection of our less desirable traits. Students who are chronic procrastinators and/or disorganized students frequently find less tolerance from teachers who recognize themselves or are recognized by their colleagues to have the offending traits. Natural tendencies slip easily into habits of mind and body. In this case, reframing requires that a teacher be able to be insightful about the thought/feeling/action pattern this student evokes.

Typical Encounter:

Mike at teacher's desk: *"Yes, I knew the project was due today. I started it on Sunday, but then we went to my cousin's house. I left it there, but when I went back to get it, some of it was missing. I had most of it in my backpack for you, but my backpack doesn't fit in my locker, so . . . I heard you gave Marisa more time."*

Ms. Baker's first thought: *"Deadlines mean something. He had plenty of time. It was a fair assignment. All those excuses are bogus! I've heard them all. Ha! I've used them all!"*

Ms. Baker's first feeling: *Disbelief, rejection, intolerance*

Ms. Baker's first action: *Refusal. No extension. Zero.*

This is a pattern that many would defend and promote as an appropriate outcome for any student. However, for the teacher who is striving to build a relationship with Mike, two questions of precedence arise. Is it more important to punish the infraction or focus on the relationship? Which is more likely to help Mike choose to change his counterproductive ways?

Realistically, "No extension" is unlikely to change Mike into a responsible student. Unfortunately, transformation is not that easy. Teaching Mike a "lesson" about the outcome of his weakness is something he already knows.

Mike's natural tendency toward disorganization and/or procrastination needs intervention and practical support. Spending some personal time with Mike to set some mutual goals for completing the project has much more potential for helping him.

A teacher whose patience has run out for Mike, but not Marisa, also has to examine if and to what degree Mike's behavior is a nagging reminder of his or her own.

Reframed Encounter:

> Ms. Baker's second thought: *"Oh, Mike . . . been there, done that. Don't do it! Deadlines mean something. Mike must learn how to organize time and accept responsibility. What can help him? Can I? I wonder."*

> Ms. Baker's second feeling: *Empathy, resolve, commitment to support the need for change.*

> Ms. Baker's second action: *An idea for a supported project plan with supported deadlines.*

> Ms. Baker: *"Yes, Mike, I did give Marisa more time. But for you, 'more time' is not a solution. Here's a plan that I hope you will like. From now on, we will meet and come up with days and times when parts of the project will be due. You can tell me how you plan to get them done, and I'll look at each part with you and grade it. You're also going to learn what mainly gets in the way of your getting things done by yourself. Maybe best of all, Mike, we'll get to know each other better. I'll like that part a lot, I think. Will you bring me the three paragraphs that describe your project tomorrow? Do you remember what each paragraph should do?"*

Numerous factors could contribute to Mike's current state of seemingly continual disorganization. For example, it may be inability to complete work on time or perhaps habitual use of prevarication to avoid responsibility. Students who display Mike's traits are high maintenance—definitely more difficult to deal with than to dismiss. They generally cause an intense level of aggravation by taxing teachers' already challenging system of assessment and record keeping. In addition, the ever-present "he needs to be responsible" mantra presents itself as a responsibility to the teacher.

This teacher displays a sophisticated level of insight into the influence that personal biases as well as personal experiences have on interactions with student issues.

- This teacher followed a cardinal rule for beginning a possible relationship with a resistant student: in a typical situation, the teacher responded differently from the student's expectation.
- This teacher demonstrated a mature and good-natured grasp of a shortcoming of her own.
- Because this teacher can draw from personal experience, the plan for support and change is likely to be realistic and well directed.
- Expressing eagerness at the prospect of knowing Mike better invites Mike to invest in the plan with additional energy derived from the motivation to please those who we perceive like us.

Example #5

Teachers who successfully form relationships with students understand the limitation of obedience to authority versus the personal growth derived from choice and responsibility.

Perhaps, for teachers, the most difficult task in establishing positive personal connections with students is learning the best way to exert authority without authoritativeness, receive respect without instilling fear, and deliver discipline without punishment.

Typical Encounter:

Mr. Devlin: *"Let's go, fourth graders! Sam, you get the kickball. Shanita, please get the jump ropes. You, Martha, will get your unfinished math and go to Ms. Thomas's class—again—because you did not finish your work—again!"*

Martha, resentfully: *"You never let me have recess!"*

Mr. Devlin's first thought: *"One of these days, that child will wake up and realize I mean business. I know she can do the work if she tries. Plenty of students in this class who are less able get their work done. She is failing for no reason."*

Mr. Devlin's first feeling: *Irritation, righteousness, conviction, weariness*

Mr. Devlin's first action: *No recess for Martha until she learns to finish her math with the others.*

When punishment has little or no effect on Martha's behavior, motivating her to work more efficiently during math class requires a different tactic. Helping Martha see that actions have consequences is a goal that could be achieved without punishment.

"You, Martha . . ." is authoritative in tone, relying on adult power for its strength. It assumes that compliance will reflect respect. The word "again," however, seems to indicate that Martha has not benefited from this punishment. More likely, Martha is feeling fearful of her teacher's clear displeasure. She attributes dislike and meanness to her teacher and resents his power. Unknowingly, the teacher has given Martha reason to blame him for the unhappy outcome of a choice that actually belongs to Martha.

Reframed Encounter:

> Mr. Devlin's second thought: *"Punishment is not working for Martha. How can I get her to improve her math grades? Where should I start now?"*
>
> Mr. Devlin's second feeling: *Perplexity, proactive control, confidence*
>
> Mr. Devlin's second action: *Devise a plan to help Martha that diminishes her resentment, creates positive interaction, and addresses the issue of unfinished math assignments.*
>
> Mr. Devlin, *before* the next math class: *"Martha, come here. How nice you look today! You know, I've been thinking about some things to help you get your math work done so you don't miss recess anymore. We miss you when you don't come out with us. Today I want you to try as hard as you can to get your work done. That's the first thing. Next, raise your hand if you get stuck, and I'll try to come right over. But you are the one who chooses to finish or not, Martha. I'm reminding you before we even start math to do the right thing. Don't waste any time at all. Will you remember to make the right choice? I hope so. Pick recess!"* (Thereafter, Mr. Devlin will keep reminding Martha that *choosing* recess is up to her.)

In this response, Mr. Devlin has begun a process that puts Martha in control of and responsible for her actions and their outcome. He has changed his role from punisher to facilitator and caring supporter. This is a very important distinction, because chances are good that Martha, habitually slow to complete her work, will still not complete it after one "pep talk."

However, beginning a new and improved relationship with Martha could motivate her to invest in change because:

- By reaching out to her in a helping, friendly fashion, the teacher responded differently from what Martha has come to expect.
- Martha has reason to doubt her judgments about whether her teacher really is mean, unfair and hateful toward her.

- The teacher has created a way to empathize with Martha when and if she doesn't complete her work—"Martha, I'm so sorry you chose not to come to recess with us today. I hope you'll choose to come tomorrow."
- The door is open for further probing/problem solving between Martha and this teacher.

For students whose social and emotional growth and development are confined by antisocial behavior, nothing is more important than relationship. The greater the antisocial confinement, the greater the need. Teachers who recognize this and believe it are the most likely ones to increase their understanding of how to offset insecure attachments, to create opportunities for belonging and to reframe their first thoughts, first feelings, and first actions.

Through the influential relationships shared with these teachers, imagined impossibilities become factual achievements. The students in their care are not lost forever. Instead, they belong. Their education builds a long-lasting foundation where self-confidence, competence, academic accomplishment, and personal pride grow and flourish.

POINTS TO REMEMBER

- Teachers *can* begin to establish positive personal connections with those who seem most unwilling, defiant, and oppositional when they understand attachment formation and the need students have to belong.
- Teachers are the *only* adults some children have to rely upon to help them cope with the consequences of their unearned circumstances outside of school.
- Students most in need show measurable improvement in their academic achievement and social growth when their teachers actively and habitually reframe negative situations into positive opportunities.

NOTES

1. Noddings, Nell. *The Challenge to Care in Schools.* New York: Teachers College Press, 1992.
2. Magid, Ken, and Carole A. McKelvey. *High Risk: Children without a Conscience.* Golden, CO: M & M Publishing, 1987.
3. Ibid.
4. Brendtro, Larry K., Martin Brokenleg, and Steve VanBockern. *Reclaiming Youth at Risk: Our Hope for the Future.* Bloomington, IN: National Education Service, 1990.
5. *The American Heritage Dictionary of the English Language,* 3rd ed., s.v. "resist."
6. Maeroff, Gene I. *Altered Destinies: Making Life Better for Children in Need.* New York: Palgrave Macmillan, 1999.
7. Kohl, Herbert. *I Won't Learn from You,* 2nd ed. New York: The New Press, 1995.

Chapter 2

Self-Talk Is Like a Message in a Bottle

> I'm nobody! Who are you?
> Are you nobody, too?
> Then there's a pair of us—don't tell!
> They'd banish us, you know.
> —*Emily Dickinson, I'm Nobody! Who Are You?* (1891)

In fable and film, when the sea delivers a message in a bottle, obvious questions capture the attention of the audience: "What is it?" "Where did it come from?" "What does it say?" "Who understands what it means?" "Will the message be life changing?" The answers to these same questions are pivotal for understanding the role self-talk plays in students who resist sincere attempts by caring teachers to form supportive relationships.

Successful attempts to establish relationships with students who resist depend upon teachers' recognition of the important role that their own self-talk plays in the process. The teachers who help students change the inner voice that calls them "nobody" to a voice that declares them "somebody" provide students as many experiences of success in school as possible. They model optimism, encouragement, and caring.

WHAT IS SELF-TALK?

Self-talk is consciously manifested internal speech, usually private rather than spoken aloud to oneself. Current researchers continue to build on the early work of Russian theorist Lev Vygotsky, who posited that one's inner speech is an essential part of cognitive development. According to Vygotsky, children around age two begin to express their thoughts with words from their language, oftentimes speaking aloud, whether or not they have some-one's attention.[1]

Sokolov asserts that thinking itself, remembering, and imagining are products of internal speech.[2] In his research on students' self-talk, Purkey constructs self as "a complex, dynamic and organized system of learned beliefs that an individual holds to be true about his or her personal exis-tence."[3]

Importantly, the daily internal conversations that direct, interpret, and explain experiences reveal the essence of a person. Inner speech guides self-perception, perceiving others, chosen work, and beliefs held about personal abilities. It influences the way relationships form and how they are main-tained or dismissed. Self-talk influences personal choices about what to learn or deliberately not learn.

As cognitive development evolves, self-talk becomes increasingly inter-nal and reflects knowledge, skills, and ways of thinking drawn from in-creased experiences. Certain situations or powerful experiences can chal-lenge long-held beliefs or convictions and even force sudden change. It is important to note that self-talk can be faulty, illogical, even irrational. It becomes habitual; it draws comfort more from familiarity than from truth. Research shows the strong connection between self-talk and personal thoughts, feelings, and actions.[4]

What does self-talk say? Sometimes it says that all is well. Most of the time self-talk helps successful navigation through a daily maze of "ups and downs." There is a healthy balance between and among conflicting events that influence physical, cognitive, social, emotional, and moral growth.

Sometimes self-talk says the opposite. Too many negative past and/or present experiences allow walls, moats, barricades, and land mines to build, deferring dreams and limiting perceived options.

The best self-talk enables an individual habitually to balance positive and negative experiences, and, while doing so, recognize and emphasize the pos-sible positive outcomes from *both* sets. Clearly, such an inner voice connects its owner to optimistic feelings about personal worth, efficacy, and ability.

Affirming self-talk influences public behavior, impacts academic achievement, enhances self-esteem, and even guards physical health. It fol-lows, then, that self-talk that habitually condemns, criticizes, accents worth-lessness, or reinforces doubt creates a thought/feeling/action pattern guaran-teed to reflect unhappiness and impact relationships at every turn.

Actions of external behaviors, which emerge from negative think/feel/act patterns, attract attention. Behaviors considered inappropriate for school quickly earn labels for transgressors. These students are the "resistant ones"—known by many names: "underachiever," "time bomb," "dropout," "dreamer," "troublemaker," "piece of work," "at risk," "passive," "aggres-sive," "passive-aggressive," to name only a few.

The actions of these students are unmistakable outward signs of their inner thoughts and feelings, leading their teachers to ask, "What is wrong here?" "Why does this student behave this way?" Unfortunately, these essential questions are usually asked in the midst of an urgent moment and remain rhetorical. Teachers who seek and find informed answers are the most likely to be able to establish healing relationships with these students.

By the time a child enters school, he or she already lives by internal dialogue that expects school to reinforce personal perceptions of self-reliance, competence, self-respect, trust, and happiness. That is, *if* the child was fortunate enough primarily to have received parental and familial warmth, respectful treatment, and well-defined behavioral limits as an infant, toddler, and preschooler.

If positive interactions and experiences have not been the norm, then inner speech reinforces feelings of self-hatred, incompetence, mistrust, and unhappiness. Such is the power of self-talk. It is cherished. Almost without warning, it can engender debate, power struggles, and staunch defense of viewpoints, right or wrong. *That is why it is so important for teachers to be very clear about the scripts they carry.* Being aware of them is the first step in becoming a teacher who can forge positive personal connections with students whose scripts may be exactly opposite to those a teacher may hold in high regard.

Building a positive personal connection with students whose life experiences to date have guaranteed mostly negative self-talk requires intentional effort, patience, and clear understanding about the strong influence self-talk has on students' view of the world. While hoping to influence their future, teachers who can build relationships must demonstrate the ability to *accept children unconditionally as they are in the present.*

Caring teachers can contribute greatly to students' self-image. It is significant others who contribute most to the formation of a positive self-image with matching self-talk. Away from home, teachers are children's most compelling influence. They can enhance every student's lived experience during the school day or reinforce whatever negativity accompanies each student who enters their classroom.

Teachers who help students strengthen their inner voice are:

- Teachers who create classroom climates that include emotional warmth.
- Teachers who know how to celebrate diversity.
- Teachers who never use humiliation, sarcasm, or teasing to control behavior.
- Teachers who know how to structure alternative, successful *experiences* to offset established, ingrained negative self-talk of students.

THE IMPACT PERSONAL SELF-TALK HAS ON STUDENTS

Consider this scenario:

> Mr. Lewis exits his classroom to find two students, unknown to him, rough-housing in the hall. Darnell and Devon, both sixth graders, are enjoying the audience that has surrounded their play. Mr. Lewis makes the judgment that injury from their antics is possible and likely. Roughhousing is quickly chang-ing to fighting. In a loud voice he tells the boys to stop. They do not. In a yet louder, more insistent voice, he commands them to stop. They ignore him. He steps forward to intervene and physically restrains Darnell by the arm. The youngster turns to him and using a string of expletives, tells Mr. Lewis to let go of him. Mr. Lewis asks the boy for his name. The boy states clearly and without equivocation that it is none of Mr. Lewis's business, calling him a "fool" in the process. Mr. Lewis disperses the watchers and ushers Darnell inside an empty classroom off the hallway. He asks the young man for his name again but only receives a hostile look and stony silence.

Self-talk affects two possible choices facing Mr. Lewis, whose responsibility it is to bring resolution to this situation:

Choice #1

Mr. Lewis's intervention in this scenario instantly forced two things to hap-pen. One, he would have had to endure a barrage of self-talk coming from within himself. It would be rooted in a number of "sacred scripts" formed from lifelong experiences that make him be the person he is today. In addi-tion, he would also be calling on "professional" teacher self-talk to bring some resolution to this dilemma.

Assume that some of Mr. Lewis's sacred scripts are these:

- Always speak respectfully to adults. (A family rule enforced by mom and dad during childhood. No exceptions.)
- Children should not engage in roughhousing. (Mr. Lewis's brother broke his arm during rough play when they were ages nine and eleven.)
- All foul language is offensive and inexcusable. (A conviction supported by church and school experience, modeled by parents and close relatives.)
- Obedience is the right of adults and the duty of children. (A family value actively promoted by Mr. Lewis in his relationship with his wife and three young children.)
- Strong teachers have few problems making children cooperate. (Classroom management class—favorite professor in master's program.)

If the above were true, an emotional, rather than a rational, response would drive Mr. Lewis's immediate and first thought/feeling/action pattern. It would be difficult to deny the many assaults on his sacred scripts presented by Darnell's behavior.

- He would draw strength from his certainty that his sacred scripts are true *(adults should be respected)*, prudent *(roughhousing can be dangerous)*, correct *(foul language is offensive)*, high-minded *(obedience is the duty of children)*, and knowledgeable *(Professor X knew what he was talking about)*.
- Roughhousing with Devon was dangerous. Injury seemed imminent, and safety is every school's priority.
- Mr. Lewis would be well within his rights to point out to Darnell that his rude and grossly disrespectful response to Mr. Lewis's intervention would result in a referral to administration, surely followed by some sort of punitive consequence.
- A detention or school suspension will fit perfectly into Darnell's expectation—desire even—of what happens when "you get in trouble."

This course of action is not "wrong" at all, should Mr. Lewis choose to use it. It is a legitimate, well-used method of managing misbehavior in schools every day at every level. Notice, though, how it is Mr. Lewis's self-talk that focuses the conversation, drives the solution, and determines the outcome. Notice, also, that a person-to-person connection between Mr. Lewis and Darnell would have to be sacrificed for an adult-to-child communication.

Choice #2

Mr. Lewis's second choice, albeit more difficult and more time consuming, would trade the quicker fix for attending to the disturbing self-talk that drove Darnell's behavior during this incident. Darnell's self-talk is clearly different from Mr. Lewis's, because it allows him to fight, swear, and express himself with such vehement anger and inappropriateness to an adult in school and, therefore, in a known role of authority.

- Mr. Lewis would first have to recognize the demands of his own self-talk and *consciously set them aside* in order to be able to focus on Darnell.
- Mr. Lewis's *concern for Darnell's obvious lack of social skill, self-control, and anger-management ability* would take precedence over Mr. Lewis's emotional reaction to Darnell's disrespect and anger.
- Mr. Lewis *would attempt a person-to-person conversation instead of an adult-to-child communication.* He would insist on it. His voice tone, body language, and word choice would display no mirroring anger or irritation. His authority would be obvious. Calm, concern, and being in absolute

control of his emotions would challenge Darnell's perception of adults because it would be *so completely different from Darnell's expectation.*

- The ultimate resolution would have to include addressing Darnell's issues, perhaps with his teacher, the school social worker, or others who might have a positive connection with Darnell. Devon's role in the incident should also be investigated. In addition, both boys should expect consequences for their behavior that satisfy school or classroom policy, but with at least some reminder about the role that choice has in determining consequences.

If Mr. Lewis chose the second option for resolving the situation with Devon and Darnell, he accomplished a lot. He engaged Darnell in conversation that recognized his self-talk and planted seeds of doubt about its effectiveness. He modeled reaction to disrespect in a way different from what Darnell had ever seen or experienced before. He offered Darnell a chance to experience a connection with an adult who did not reinforce Darnell's perception of adults as non-helpers.

COUNTERACT STUDENTS' NEGATIVE SELF-TALK—FIVE EXAMPLES

Consider the students whose self-talk is rooted in life experiences drawn mainly from one of these: violence, physical abuse, sexual abuse, neglect, and/or poverty. Resistant students who demonstrate at-risk behaviors are often unfortunate recipients of one or even *all five* of these negative life experiences. Each one of these factors provides scripts of influence that can and often do last a lifetime.

Research, case studies, personal accounts, and court transcripts all bear witness to the destructive thought/feeling/action patterns that emerge from experiences beyond students' control and ability to understand. Whether or not internal dialogue is accurate, factually right, or factually wrong, it serves a purpose: it permits actions to follow from thoughts and feelings consonant with one's experience.

Changing established patterns of self-talk does not occur quickly. The initial disequilibrium it creates is unsettling and creates doubt about the trustworthiness of the new perception that challenges the old perception.

In order to influence students to change their negative self-talk, teachers must:

- Set aside personal scripts that interfere with focusing insightful attention on the self-talk of the student.

- Recognize the negative self-talk that students use to undermine their positive potential.
- Provide *experiences* for students that are different from those that drive their negative self-talk. This causes internal conflict that forces students to consider altering the self-talk that contrasts with their current experience.
- Model positive social skills, optimistic outlooks, and enthusiastic actions, consciously and consistently.

The following examples suggest actions teachers might take to counteract students' self-talk, ingrained through negative life experiences:

Example #1

Life Experience: Violence

Violence sows seeds of self-talk students use to hide, protect themselves, release anger, and wend their way in a world perceived as unfriendly.

Student Background:

Well-known, long-standing neighborhood and family violence

Incident: Grade 8

On Monday morning, Mr. Borland saw William slap Greg on the side of his head when Greg hesitated to give William a pencil and some loose-leaf paper. He snatched the items from Greg and laughed as he walked away. This is typical of William's bullying behavior. Mr. Borland kept William after class to address the behavior he witnessed. At first, William acted indifferent. When pressed by Mr. Borland's insistence on addressing William's behavior, he became hostile, denying, and argumentative.

Self-talk Mr. Borland had to set aside:

"I know what I saw."

"I still remember being bullied by Joey N."

"Children should never raise their voice to an adult."

"I'm not giving up my free time to be ignored by a bully. Forget this."

"I wish I could give him a taste of his own medicine!"

William's self-talk:

"I'm tough."

"Life is short."

"Be strong."

"Hurt others before they hurt you."

"My reputation gives me power."

William's expectation:

Mr. Borland will lecture me about being "nice" to others and respectful to teachers.

Mr. Borland will tell me, "This behavior has got to stop!"

Mr. Borland will call my mother. She won't care. I don't.

Mr. Borland will threaten me with a referral for my bad behavior.

Mr. Borland will be sorry he messed with me, because I don't take anything from anybody.

Teachers do not understand the "real" world or appreciate what I've been through.

Mr. Borland's action:

Mr. Borland recognized that negative self-talk was driving William's bullying behavior. He resolved to try to make a positive personal connection with William by creating some opportunities for William to experience some success in school. He hoped to offset some of William's obvious self-doubt, fear, need for control, and unhappiness.

- As soon as William became hostile and argumentative, Mr. Borland told William that he disliked arguments of any kind, especially with students, so it would be better to talk at a different time. He dismissed William but thanked him for trying to listen.
- In class, after lunch, Mr. Borland made it a point to call on William for an answer in math (William's best subject), to walk by his desk and make a positive comment about his work.
- As William headed for the bus after school, Mr. Borland asked William if he would meet with him during the next day's lunch period. William said, "No." Mr. Borland said, "OK."

- Later that week, Mr. Borland phoned William's mother to say that he was pleased to see William doing well in math (the only subject he was passing). He did not focus on the other failing grades.
- The next week, Mr. Borland asked William if he would be willing to help Tasha with two math problems that Mr. Borland knew William could do. William agreed. Mr. Borland then had occasion to thank William sincerely for doing that, demonstrating his belief in William's ability as well.
- Two weeks after the "incident," with more such incidents still ongoing, Mr. Borland asked William if he would stop by after school. When William said, "OK." Mr. Borland knew he had made some progress in establishing a connection with William.
- At that meeting, Mr. Borland continued to behave differently from William's expectation. Mr. Borland asked William what he liked to do, what his "favorites" were, and what he thought might be a good job to have. William had few conversations like this with anyone, especially a teacher. At the end of their meeting, Mr. Borland made gentle reference to the "trouble" that seemed to be William's partner in school. Mr. Borland told William he had some ideas about how William could use his power better. William agreed to talk with Mr. Borland again.

Example #2

Life Experience: Physical Abuse

Visible and invisible scars mark the lives of children who suffer physical abuse from caretakers or authority figures who are supposed to provide love, security, nurturing, and guidance. The self-talk of these children smolders with anger and sadness, frequently promoting both aggression and passivity.

Student Background:

Physical abuse a frequent occurrence at home; police reports, hospital visits, temporary foster care placements, restraining orders, and so on, are all part of Tierra's and her sister's direct experience.

Incident: Grade 6

Tierra missed her English class unit test because she met with a Child Protective Services worker at school. In explaining her absence, laughingly she told Ms. Wilding that over the weekend, she and her sister were placed at the Children's Shelter because Franco, Tierra's stepfather, "went crazy" again and hit them with a broom handle because they were arguing about doing the dishes. When their mother intervened, Franco knocked her to the floor in the scuffle and kicked her in the stomach. She said the police came, which was why they were sent to the shelter, but they were back home again. Ms. Wilding said, "What a bad experience! What about the unit test you missed?" Tierra rolled her eyes and said, "What about it? Who cares?"

Self-talk Ms. Wilding had to set aside:

"Physical abuse has no place in a civilized society."

"Women who let men dominate them are weak."

"I am tired of hearing these pathetic stories. It's always something with her."

"Thank goodness Child Protective Services is already involved. I won't have to be."

"So many people don't know how to get out of their own way."

Tierra's self-talk:

"Don't show when you're hurt."

"It's normal for parents to hit their kids."

"It's no big deal to fight with someone who annoys you."

"It may be wrong to hurt someone, but everybody does it."

Tierra's expectation:

Ms. Wilding is nice but clueless.

Ms. Wilding will make me make up the work I missed.

Ms. Wilding doesn't care about what kids like me go through.

Ms. Wilding's action:

Tierra's story sheds even more light on Ms. Wilding's observations about her. Tierra's readiness to fight over "he said/she said" gossip and just about everything else has natural roots. During the class's discussion of *Where the Red Fern Grows* by Wilson Rawls, Tierra's comment that Billy should "get over it" when he mourned the tragic loss of his dogs comes to Ms. Wilding's mind. It seemed so callous then but more understandable now. Ms. Wilding resolves to make a special effort to encourage Tierra over the next few months, hoping to make her time in school more positive and peaceful.

- Every morning after the incident, without fail, Ms. Wilding said, "Good morning. How are you, Tierra?" Sometimes she would compliment her hair or dress.
- Ms. Wilding asked Tierra to have lunch with her. When she accepted the invitation, Ms. Wilding asked Tierra what her favorite kind of ice cream treat was and brought it to the lunch date.
- When Tierra was in one of her obvious fighting moods, Ms. Wilding would ask her what was wrong. She would try to dissuade her from actions that would get her suspended. She would truly listen and express concern for Tierra's welfare, assuring her that she would be missed if she were to be suspended from school because of fighting.
- One time, Ms. Wilding brought a small poster that had a poem about peace and love on it. She gave it to Tierra to use as she wished, mentioning that Ms. Wilding had one just like it in her home office.
- As their relationship grew, Tierra talked to Ms.Wilding as often as time allowed. More and more often, she came before or after school. Ms. Wilding made sure Tierra felt welcome every time and gave her her undivided attention or explained why she could not do so. Ms. Wilding encouraged Tierra to use the help offered by the school social worker as well as the caseworker from Child Protective Services. Tierra behaved better in Ms. Wilding's class than in any other.

Example #3

Life Experience: Sexual Abuse

Sexually abused children experience emotional and psychological scars that can interfere with their daily functioning well into their adult years. The trauma sexual abuse causes is so great that it does not end when the abuse stops; it only marks the beginning of a long road to recovery.

Student Background:

Sonia lives with her mother, father, older brother, and younger sister. They recently moved into a new house in a very nice neighborhood. Both parents work to maintain the comfortable living standards they enjoy. Sonia and her siblings are responsible students who enjoy school and extracurricular activities.

Incident: Grade 9

Sonia was the first one out of health class the day Mrs. Hurst had a guest speaker make a presentation on sexual abuse. Mrs. Hurst noticed that during the talk, try as she might, Sonia was unable to disguise her discomfort. She would look down and around, tap her foot, jiggle in her chair, and, then, become perfectly still. The next day, Sonia's friend Anita told Mrs. Hurst that Sonia said that her father should be the one having "sex talks" about abuse. Mrs. Hurst thanked Anita for telling her and said she would look into it.

Aware that she was required to report incidents of sexual abuse, Mrs. Hurst spoke with the school social worker that day and was shocked to learn that the family was already under investigation due to a previously reported incident.

Self-talk Mrs. Hurst had to set aside:

"Sonia is such a moody girl—she is difficult to like."

"Family secrets should never be aired in public."

"Incest is the worst crime in the world."

"Avoidance is the best and kindest treatment for embarrassing situations."

Sonia's self-talk:

"My father really loves me."

"What's happening is wrong."

"Trust no adult."

"It's my fault."

"I would hurt my mother if I told the truth."

Sonia's expectation:

Mrs. Hurst would never believe me if I told her about my life.

I don't know anyone at school who knows Mrs. Hurst.

Mrs. Hurst has never been really nice to me before. Be careful.

Mrs. Hurst's action:

Mrs. Hurst resolved to try to provide some experiences that might boost Sonia's self-esteem. By interacting with Sonia more, Mrs. Hurst created a few positive personal connections. She began by asking Sonia to help her put up a bulletin board for health class, knowing it would provide a chance to get to know Sonia outside of class.

- So that she could offer Sonia legitimate praise for her work, Mrs. Hurst regularly asked Sonia to help put up the classroom bulletin boards or make charts, and so on.
- Mrs. Hurst remembered Sonia's birthday with a card and small gift.
- Mrs. Hurst looked up Sonia's report card after each marking period and wrote her a note of congratulation and/or encouragement about her grades.
- As freshman class moderator, Mrs. Hurst asked Sonia, an excellent reader, to read a poem during the Freshman Class Talent Show in the Spring.
- For the rest of the year, Mrs. Hurst smiled at Sonia often, commented on her clothes or makeup, and tried to engage her in simple conversations.

Example #4

Life Experience: Poverty

Poverty is a condition that can undermine children's security and self-esteem in such a way as to convince them they are destined to be inferior and at angry odds with anyone who has more privilege.

Student Background:

The youngest of six children, Charles's father is unemployed and his mother works part-time. His family has been evicted four times for not paying rent. Charles's family has been on public assistance since he was born. His only relatives, two aunts and one uncle, live in Tennessee.

Incident: Grade 4

It happened that *all* twenty-two fourth-grade students received 100 percent on the unit test in spelling. Charles folded the paper with a number on it, waiting anxiously for the drawing to take place. As a surprise reward, Ms. Hunt managed to snare an inexpensive but smart-looking MP3 player. It was a coveted prize. Suzanne won, choosing a number just one away from Charles's choice. Ms. Hunt noticed that Charles was clearly upset; it was painful to see him appear so desperate to win. Much later, in math class, he was still muttering to himself, frowning and punching his thigh in frustration and disappointment. Trying to be sympathetic, Ms. Hunt called Charles to her desk while the class was at work. She said, "I can tell you really wanted to win that MP3 player Charles, and . . ." Charles responded angrily, "No! I really don't care!" He turned on his heel and walked back to his desk.

Self-talk Ms. Hunt had to set aside:

"Always appreciate someone else's kindness."

"Winning isn't everything; losing strengthens your spirit."

"Poor losers are immature and annoying."

"Never place too much value on material goods."

Charles's self-talk:

"Nothing good ever happens to me."

"I want . . . but I'll never get it."

"Everything is unfair."

"Everybody is always showing off."

"Don't worry about me—I take care of myself."

Charles's expectation:

Ms. Hunt is always telling us, "Good luck!" There's no such thing.

Ms. Hunt doesn't have to feel sorry for me.

Ms. Hunt doesn't know anything about me.

Ms. Hunt is just another teacher. That's all.

Ms. Hunt's action:

Ms. Hunt thought about Charles's reaction to losing the drawing and his response to her attempt to extend sympathy. She thought how urgency, indifference, hostility, and pessimism frequently attended both Charles's accomplishments and his relationships. Ms. Hunt resolved to be intentional about offering Charles more opportunities to experience optimism while in school.

- Ms. Hunt found out more about Charles's background from last year's teacher.
- Ms. Hunt started putting stickers on everyone's schoolwork. She also wrote short messages on Charles's work to let him know she saw something good in everything he did.
- Ms. Hunt called on Charles more and sent him to the board more often, praising his writing, his effort, or his posture.

- When she knew Charles did not have necessary supplies, she would bring two or three of what was needed and ask the whole class, "Who wants these extra folders (or . . .) I have?" Sparing Charles the embarrassment of being singled out, she would give them away, making sure he was a recipient.
- Ms. Hunt wrote a few positive notes home about something good that Charles did, hoping Charles's mom would perceive her as an advocate. Then, in a separate note, Ms. Hunt told Charles's mother that she realized raising six children was a very big task. She explained that sometimes people offered items such as dishes, towels, or clothing items to schools for people with large families, inviting Charles's mother to stop by or write a note if she could use items like that.
- Ms. Hunt created writing assignments for the entire fourth grade that often focused on favorite things, a happy memory, or things to appreciate, hoping to help Charles think more positively.

Example #5

Life Experience: Neglect

Neglect wears many costumes, hiding itself in the complexity of subjective judgment, perception, customs, and cultural practices. General agreement is that neglect results from consistent failure on the part of the caretaker responsible for safeguarding a child's emotional and physical health and well-being.

Student Background:

Numerous contacts to parents left unanswered. Frequent lateness and absence from school. Several appointments for home visits canceled.

Incident: Grade 2

The newspaper headline read *LATE NIGHT ARRESTS SURPRISE NEIGHBORS.* The accompanying picture showed police officers escorting four people in handcuffs from the house. Mr. Clausen recognized Dana's mother and stepfather. An immediate mental video of Dana played in his mind: Dana at his desk chewing on bits of paper, Dana being separated from Seth in a playground fight, Dana faltering in his reading group, Dana unkempt and unhappy.

He expected this incident would eventually add to an already too-fat permanent record file for Dana, detailing a history of family dysfunction that explained but did not resolve the anger and resentment, hopelessness and helplessness that characterized Dana in school.

Self-talk Mr. Clausen had to set aside:

"The world is full of trouble, most of it by people's own making."

"A teacher's job is to teach. Only."

"Some children are damaged beyond repair."

"The welfare system is mainly a drain on taxpayers' dollars."

Dana's self-talk:

"I can do whatever I want."

"Nobody really cares."

"I know lots of ways to get attention if I want it."

"I'll hurt you before you hurt me."

Dana's expectation:

Mr. Clausen? He's just my teacher.

Schoolwork is hard. I don't like it.

Mr. Clausen is always bossing us around.

The principal's office is pretty. It's got nice chairs and a blue rug.

Mr. Clausen's action:

Mr. Clausen decided to try to provide Dana with experiences of caring to offset the lack of caring that has seemed so apparent in his life outside of school.

- Mr. Clausen spoke directly and kindly to Dana every day.
- The principal agreed to let Dana come to her office for "Happy Visits"; Mr. Clausen manufactured as many as he honestly could.
- Mr. Clausen started a "Lunch Bunch," inviting a small group of students to eat in the classroom with him once a week and to enjoy a small treat he provided. Frequently he included Dana.
- Whenever Mr. Clausen chose spontaneously to reward children for good work or behavior, he would try to make the paper or pencil or star or

sticker for Dana be red, knowing it was his favorite color. He would call Dana's attention to that little act of thoughtfulness.

* Mr. Clausen faithfully exercised greater patience and calm when dealing with Dana's misbehavior.
* Mr. Clausen arranged for some tutorial help for some of his poorest readers by working out a plan with the eighth-grade teacher and two willing and able students. Dana was one of the first students to get some one-on-one attention in this way.

Perhaps the best "message in a bottle" from the sea of self-talk is that teachers who understand the power of self-talk can be an enormous influence on the children in their care. Every intentional action taken by a teacher to drown the voices that tell students they are "nobody" is also an invitation to relationship, everyone's anchor for a healthy life.

POINTS TO REMEMBER

* Students' actions resulting from self-talk are unmistakable outward signs of their inner thoughts and feelings about themselves and others. Self-talk influences beliefs, true or false, about abilities, personal choices, and all relationships.
* Throughout the school day, teachers' actions contribute to students' formation of a positive self-image with matching self-talk, or they reinforce whatever negative self-talk students carry.
* Teachers who can build relationships must demonstrate the ability to *accept children unconditionally as they are in the present.*
* It is essential that teachers are aware of the sources and strength of their own self-talk.
* Changing self-talk and resulting behaviors does not occur quickly; admonitions fail—only *experiences that challenge held perceptions* effect change.

NOTES

1. Vygotsky, L. S. *The Genetic Roots of Thinking and Speech.* In Anita Woolfolk, *Educational Psychology* (p. 45). Upper Saddle River, NJ: Pearson Education, Inc., 2010.
2. Sokolov, A. N. *Inner Speech and Thought.* New York: Plenum, 1972.
3. Purkey, William Watson. *What Students Say to Themselves.* Thousand Oaks, CA: Corwin Press, 2000.
4. Bandura, Albert. *Social Foundations of Thought and Action.* Upper Saddle River, NJ: Prentice Hall, 1986.

Chapter 3

Do Battles Win Wars?

I always say that, next to a battle lost, the greatest misery is a battle gained.
—*Duke of Wellington, British general and statesman (1769–1852)*

History attests to the high personal, environmental, and financial cost of battles won. When a battle represents a win unrelated to the cause it was designed to support, the win, paradoxically, is actually a loss. In education, the ongoing contests between and among myriad forces that affect the lives of children in the system at any given time frequently use the analogy of war.

The purpose of the "war" in education is to assist as many students as possible in the positive development of who they are and who they can become. Teachers who do not lose sight of the purpose of the war willingly offer students the kind of relationship from which they can draw strength along the way. In particular, conflict, developmental challenges, and power struggles are minefields that teachers maneuver successfully in support of students' cognitive, social, moral, and physical growth.

RECOGNIZE CONFLICT AS OPPORTUNITY

When opportunity knocks, open the door! It is a notion that creates a positive mental picture in most people—a wide-open sunny gateway, ushering in surprising fame or good fortune. When conflict comes calling, the welcome is less enthusiastic, to be sure. Some retreat instead, whereas others gather strength for the onslaught and its after-effects. Still others reach for people or things that might help them withstand the storm.

The paradox is that conflict should have the door open widest; stress, tension, cognitive confusion, and life crises are reliable predictors of personal growth and harbingers of necessary change. Countless phrases attest to this and serve to help us draw courage for each day's challenges. For example, the "night darkest before the dawn," where we have "been tried as gold in a furnace" and "made stronger by infirmity" tells us that "no pain means no gain" as we "look for the silver lining."

It requires notable insight and skill during the course of a busy school day to see conflict as an opportunity. Conflict is "a state of disharmony between incompatible persons or persons whose ideas or interests clash. It is a mental struggle resulting from mutually exclusive impulses, desires, or tendencies."[1] It is not surprising, then, that by its nature, conflict engages emotions much more quickly than reason.

Conflict occurs in classrooms every day. Resistant students usually encounter trouble in school. Very often after phone calls home, visits to the principal's office, punishments, or several suspensions from school, students' negative behaviors lessen—at least temporarily.

This hiatus from bad behavior is a fragile time when resistant students are both more vulnerable and more receptive to change. This is the time when teachers' attempts to make a positive personal connection can help students recognize that they have power to make different choices. When a crisis brings a student to a crossroads, teachers need only take care that their intervention improves or at least leaves things the same. The maxim to which doctors ascribe, "at least, do no harm," also applies to teachers.

The experiences of students that do not lead to growth perpetuate irrational beliefs that cement negative self-talk. Teacher responses based on emotional reactions to student behavior driven by a student's emotional reactions perpetuate a cycle that honors conflict for its own sake. Intervention is necessary to stop the cycle.

Three convictions about conflict that strengthen a teacher's ability to form positive relationships with all students, even the most resistant, are:

1. Conflict is an opportunity for growth or change.
2. Correct application of authority frequently can stop power struggles with students before they start.
3. Conflict is cyclical.

The following two examples shed light on what happens when conflict is an unproductive cycle. Intervening differently from what a student expects by breaking the conflict cycle facilitates the opportunity for growth or change.

Example #1—Grade 1

Kathy and Kaleesha engage in name-calling every day. The "names" they call each other are frightful—rude, derogatory, insulting, and frequently accompanied by obscene gestures. Sometimes they laugh when they do it; other times, anger and hostility prevail. Both seem equally at fault. If one doesn't start, the other will.

Kathy and Kaleesha, at the young age of five or six, have learned from observation and direct experience about name-calling. They have heard others say the names they say, they know name-calling affects the recipient, gets reaction from their peers, and likely elicits an immediate, attentive response from their teacher.

It is possible that these young girls are simply enjoying the act of adult mimicry. It is also possible that these children already feel driven by self-talk that compels them to behave in ways that are hurtful to others. True to human nature, a teacher's first *inner* response to the girls' engaging in such inflammatory name-calling will be emotional. Any adult would rightfully be saddened, shocked, dismayed, or troubled by it.

The most common teacher intervention is using words and body language to register displeasure (drawn from his or her emotional reaction) at Kathy and Kaleesha's behavior. Doing this models behavior that reinforces whatever negativity Kathy and Kaleesha already feel is necessary to interact with others. Generally, this follows an application of authority that admonishes the girls, forbids them to repeat their offense, and threatens punishment.

An intervention that capitalizes on *conflict as an opportunity for growth or change* is different in this way: A teacher will recognize that his or her first response is emotional and should not direct the outward way he or she chooses to address the girls' inappropriate behavior. Instead, skilled teachers explore behavior-changing interventions that rely on reason, insight, and long-range influence.

In this incident, Kathy and Kaleesha's teacher would exercise intentional emotional control when confronting them about their unacceptable behavior. Patience, openness, pleasantness, and warmth would mark their interaction. Their teacher might choose to help them think of complimentary or funny names that they could call each other, while investigating why they have the need to name-call at all. The girls' interaction with their teacher will be positive, friendly, and reinforce an alternative model for relating to others.

Each time the girls engage in name-calling, the teacher's intervention should be the same. When the unwanted behavior begins to abate even a little, the teacher should notice immediately and offer praise to the girls separately and collectively. Over time, the teacher could continue to reinforce the desired behavior, perhaps by featuring the meaning or origin of every child's name in the class.

Example #2—Grade 4

Jonathan insists on bringing an array of electronic games to school and attempts to play them during class time, causing distraction and annoyance. When one is taken away, another appears from a seemingly endless supply.

In this example, the usual intervention—dealing with Jonathan's disregard for rules pertaining to attentive and participatory learning by taking away the object of distraction—appears to be having little or no effect, as he continues to bring more toys to school. A number of things, ranging from worrisome to routine, could be behind his lack of cooperation—simple immaturity about embracing the rigors of academic study, a hope to gain peer acceptance by impression, a learning disability, a need for attention or resentment toward authority, to name a few.

The teacher who can change this irksome classroom conflict into an opportunity for Jonathan's growth will use the intervention technique that keeps his or her emotional response hidden from Jonathan. He will not feel the irritation and annoyance the teacher feels. Instead, before taking the toy away, the teacher should try to start the conversation with Jonathan by showing interest in his possession of and dexterity with his games.

Later, after deciding whether the root of his behavior is cause for concern, the teacher could begin to establish a connection with Jonathan by asking to learn how to play one of the confiscated games after school. Creating a positive connection, however it happens, promises Jonathan's teacher a sphere of influence, which is the best way to gain Jonathan's willing cooperation regarding toys during class time. As much as possible, Jonathan should be part of a plan for reform.

In both examples cited, the teacher may or may not discover *exactly* what is causing the unwanted behavior. However, the teacher who chose to *interrupt* the conflict cycle made a positive personal connection. Connections with their teachers influence students by casting a new and different light on counterproductive behavior cycles.

CAPITALIZE ON DEVELOPMENTAL CHALLENGES

Most psychology textbooks feature Erik Erikson's work on human psychosocial development. His theory posits that throughout eight stages of personal and emotional development, marking birth to advanced old age, a number of age-related tasks, opportunities, or dilemmas occur as part of daily living that determine the degree of self-actualization a person attains. [2]

Subsequent research pertaining to these tasks or dilemmas, which Erikson calls "crises," has revealed considerable flexibility and diversity between and among the periods of development Erikson outlines. Nonetheless, Erikson's stage theory continues to provide a general idea of the ages and life events most likely especially to impact the personal and emotional development of children.

For example, the main events for children during their school years center on becoming more independent, success in school, and building positive peer relationships. Actual or vicarious life experiences that allow exposure, modeling, encouragement, and support enable development of a healthy self-image and positive view of others. In addition, cognitive, moral, and physical milestones measure development during each stage.

If, during the years of formative growth, more negative than positive experiences occur, the foundation that supports a healthy personality is weak. Then negative self-talk colors perspective. Through each stage of development, when ethical questions, moral dilemmas, and social interactions arise, they are subject to interpretations viewed through a negative lens.

Teachers who can recognize developmental "crises" in students *and* see these markers as opportunities for personal growth or behavior change are priceless. The relationships they form and the practical guidance and encouragement they offer genuinely affect the present and future lives of students in their care.

Many teachers contend that no stage is more fraught with challenge and emotion than the one that marks an adolescent's transition from childhood to young adulthood. The span of years in this period, ages twelve to eighteen, covers an extensive range of maturation milestones and life experiences.

An adolescent who arrives at the end stage of this period with a sense of purpose, self-identity, moral code, and community awareness will have, more often than not, successfully managed the challenges they encountered. Books have been written, stories told, and memories endure that involve the essential, sometimes life-saving role teachers of adolescent students play during this time.

Countless unwritten thank-you notes live in the hearts of adults who received gifts of time, generosity, and personal attention from teachers when they were adolescents. Some notes actually written typify some of the age-related tasks and/or serious dilemmas middle- and high-school students face daily.

Dear Mr. R,

Thank you for helping me find ways to pay for the trip to Spain and talking to my grandpa about it. I'm really excited. It will be my first time far away from home. Being with so many of my friends will make it so much fun. Mrs. A gave me a camera. I'll show you the pictures.

V.

Teacher Recognized: Need for independence, importance of peer influence, opportunity for a wider worldview, financial need

Dear Mrs. Z.,

Happy Anniversary! Do you remember me? My birthday and your anniversary are on the same day. I'm eighteen today and now Myra is six. We're still together, she's doing great. I'm not married and don't have anyone right now. I'm working part-time at a supermarket and getting my GED. I want to thank you for sticking by me when I told you about being pregnant in 7th grade. I still wonder why you were so nice to me when I was so mean to everybody else, even you. My apartment is near the hospital and that Burger King. Myra loves french fries; when we're there I remember all the times we went there after my doctor's appointments. I hope you're ok and that this finds you at school. I still hate my mother. I had to say it.

B.

Teacher Recognized: Risk-taking behavior, emotional insecurity, poor impulse control, need for adult intervention and anger-management modeling

Coach M.,

I got accepted at Pittsburgh!!! I never would have been able to get in if you didn't help me write that essay or get Mr. T. to help me with Math on Saturdays. All the rough times are worth it now. I know that I owe you thanks for being tough on me.

J.

Teacher Recognized: Academic weakness, disorganization, self-discipline, and self-confidence issues

Dear Ms. B.,

My mother told me she tried to contact you to tell you about my art show in Moscow, but your number changed. I'm writing this to school, hoping you'll get it somehow, even though I know you're not there anymore. Mrs. B., you were the first teacher who encouraged me to develop my talent in art and who put up with my immature behavior in tenth grade. I can never thank you enough for believing in me, even after I got thrown out of that special summer program for being AWOL. You worked so hard to get me that scholarship. How dumb I was! I have my own studio in New York now and I'm 34 years old! I have crafted this ceramic bluebird for you because you really were "the bluebird on my shoulder" back then. All the best to you, Ms. B.

E.

Teacher Recognized: Unusual talent, risk-taking behavior, lack of familial role models, mistrust of adults, stubbornness, strong self-will

In every case, the teachers in these examples chose an option that involved building a relationship with a student as a way to help that student meet the challenges encountered as an adolescent.

Some situations were classically routine; others were crises that affected the lives of those students forever. The ability to be generous, kind, open, nonjudgmental, and selfless are some of the dispositions common to teachers who are memorable to their students. In a similar way, many students who are memorable to their teachers also could (and maybe do) receive notes of thanks for providing their teachers enrichment, satisfaction, and joy far beyond their professional expectation.

PREVENT UNNECESSARY POWER STRUGGLES

Teachers and students know well what happens during a power struggle. Conflict rules. Whether the issue at hand is grave or minor, the same dynamics are at work. Authority is questioned. Authority is challenged.

The progression of a conflict cycle can and usually does move at lightning speed. Only teachers who have learned to recognize the pattern can change the conflict cycle to a coping cycle.

A stressful incident, major or minor, occurs.

Teacher: *"Do this."*

Student: *"I don't have to do that."*

Teacher: *"Please, do this now."*

Student: *"I won't do that."*

Negative thoughts trigger feelings.
Both teacher and student self-talk demands allegiance to the core values and beliefs related to the issue.

Teacher's thoughts: *"I know what's best here. I am in charge. Children should always obey their elders. Now the whole class will realize I mean business. Disrespect should be punished. This child needs discipline."*

Student's thoughts: *"I'm nobody's slave. Don't boss me around. I am in charge of myself. I do what I want to do. Adults are against kids. Teachers do not understand anything."*

Emotions, *not* reason, drive behavior. Therefore, response is reactive.

Teacher: *"You will do this, immediately."*

Student: *"I will not do it!"*

Bad behavior incites adult. *If the adult fails to control counteraggressive feelings, this is the point of no return.* The power struggle will move forward, and the adult will need to rely on authority to resolve the issue. The adult will win the struggle.

Adult mirrors the behavior of the student.

Teacher: *"Do this, or you will regret not doing it."*

Student: *"Do what you need to do, but I'll make you regret it."*

Teacher does whatever it takes to win contest of wills (writes referral, sends for sentry, forces compliance).

Student's self-fulfilling prophecy is reinforced.

Student's thoughts: *"Same old story. Teachers should get a life. All they want is power. Too bad she can't teach math so I can get it. I'll never graduate."*

Teacher's thoughts: *"This wastes so much of my time, but it's over now."*

Time to process the incident is usually limited.

Teacher: *"I hope we won't have to go through this again."*

Student: *"Whatever."*

When a student confronts a teacher in a power struggle, is it an unacceptable affront to that teacher's authority? Sometimes, but not always. The power struggles settled by the use of authority and blind obedience are not difficult to determine.

It bears repeating that egregious public disrespect, threats to the safety of the class, violent actions, or serious threats of violence against the teacher call for immediate and strong use of authority without equivocation. However, such power challenges are not generally the ones that steal teaching time and cause daily dilemmas for teachers who try to build relationships with their students.

Knowing how to differentiate between necessary and unnecessary power struggles is possibly one of the most useful teacher techniques. In class, when teachers make a conscious effort to stop power struggles from escalating, it saves instruction time. In addition, whenever teachers decide to avoid power struggles, students are left to question their belief that teachers routinely use their power to settle differences without regard for the true facts or feelings about a situation. Masterful classroom managers are:

- Teachers who realize that the true nature of their authority as adults in charge of children is for the purpose of providing structure for their school day by guaranteeing safety, security, order, predictability, and effective instruction.

  Marvin, a well-known "skipper," was sitting on the open railing in the stairwell between the second and third floor, during class time, wearing a hat on his head. (Concern for his safety alone gave the teacher who came upon him the right and responsibility to speak to him.)

- Teachers who realize that normal development creates a need for independence in children. Without it, they cannot internalize self-discipline, responsibility, or self-confidence. These teachers recognize that guided independence is different from complete freedom or blind obedience.

  Marvin did not like to be constrained by rules of any kind. He could refuse to conform, and he was good at it; he could not do academic work, and he was routinely unsuccessful.

- Teachers who are self-aware by habit; they know what personal baggage they carry and why. They are conscious of the different ways it creates self-talk that drives their behavior and determines what they do, how they think, and how they interact with students.

  Mrs. Flint is a compliant person. In childhood, she discovered it was best to be that way to please her strict dad and dominating mom. Now, as an adult, she personally thinks the world would be a better place if more people would stop arguing and do what they are told. On the other hand, she admits that there is merit in disagreement and diversity, and she is trying to be more assertive when expressing her convictions at school committee meetings.

  When Mrs. Flint encountered Marvin, one thought tumbled after the other in rapid succession: "Marvin—skipping again. He could fall off the railing and really get hurt. That child thinks he can do whatever he wants. He's such a bully. He knows not to wear that hat. I'm in for an unpleasant confrontation. I should have used the other stairway. This kid never does what he's told. He's not my kid, anyway. I wonder what's wrong with him. Where are the sentries when you need them?"

- Teachers who are able to resist using an emotional response as a *first* response to behavior that challenges their authority. They send as few challenge messages as possible by avoiding eye contact and allowing ample personal space. They realize the limited benefit of coercion and control.

  Mrs. Flint: *"Hi, Marvin."*

Marvin: No response. No movement.

Mrs. F., pleasantly, no menacing looks, careful of personal space, smiling: *"You know you should be in class . . . please take off your hat, Marvin. I . . ."*

Marvin, angrily: *"I ain't taking this off!"*

- Teachers who can keep things in perspective; they can "lighten up," use humor, back away from a contest of wills that they think is not worth their energy. They know when the struggle might cause a negative outcome that outweighs compliance or when their relationship (or prospect of one) with a student or class should take precedence over all.

Mrs. Flint, pausing, looking at Marvin pleasantly: *"OK."*

Mrs. Flint could see no influential outcome from the contest before her. She decided to use her old friend, avoidance, to deal with it.

Marvin: No immediate comment. Definitely a surprised look.

Mrs. Flint started down the stairs.

Marvin: *"Hey, Miss. What's your name?"*

Mrs. Flint, pausing, turning, speaking with exactly the same inflection Marvin used, but smiling: *"I ain't telling you my name!"*

Marvin, with ever so slight a smile: *"OK."*

The next day, Mrs. Flint saw Marvin in the hall during the change of classes. To her surprise, a smiling Marvin said, "Hey, Miss." By choosing not to engage in a power struggle with Marvin on the previous day, and by using humor that came naturally to her, Mrs. Flint presented herself to Marvin differently from what he expected. His "hello" the next day was an indicator that Mrs. Flint had a much better chance at a positive interaction with Marvin in the future, if she had occasion to pursue it. She never did.

By virtue of their position, teachers "win" power struggles. However, the war is not really about the battle. It is, rather, about students' struggle to win the war within them. Helping students win *that* war does not happen by winning power struggles that are actually inconsequential in the grand scheme of things. Many battles simply represent the need students have to change whatever prevents them from becoming the best persons they can be. Relationship is a better battle cry.

POINTS TO REMEMBER

- Teacher responses based on emotional reactions to student behavior driven by a student's emotional reactions perpetuate a cycle that honors conflict for its own sake. No one wins such a power struggle.
- Teachers who recognize developmental markers can capitalize on the opportunities for growth they present by using them to offer students chances to experience positive personal connections that challenge negative self-talk.
- Knowing how to differentiate between necessary and unnecessary power struggles saves time, models emotional control and mature conflict-management skills, and maximizes students' trust in their teacher's ability to safeguard peace in the classroom community.

NOTES

1. *The American Heritage Dictionary of the English Language*, 3rd ed., s.v. "conflict."
2. Erikson, E. H. *Childhood in Society*, 2nd ed. New York: Norton, 1963. In Anita Woolfolk, *Educational Psychology* (p. 17). Upper Saddle River, NJ: Pearson Education, Inc., 2010.

Chapter 4

This Fire Needs Water!

Speak when you are angry, and you will make the best speech you will ever regret.
—Ambrose Bierce, *The Devil's Dictionary*

The positive connotation of the word aggression describes a person bold and active, full of enterprise and initiative. It is not that association, however, that engages the public agenda and causes teachers concern and unprecedented challenge at every education level. Frequently, advice on how to handle aggression is taught to children by loving parents at an early age: "Don't let anyone hit you! If they do, hit them right back!," "Never be anyone's door-mat!," "If you use that tone of voice with me again, I'll knock you from here to Sunday!" It is a common belief that responding to anger with anger will show strength, power, assertiveness, and control.

ANGER MANAGEMENT IN THE CLASSROOM

Students who manifest aggressive behavior are so difficult to teach in a classroom because their anger tends to bring out anger in everyone else. It is helpful when teachers can remember that aggression is a *learned* behavior, which, like so many others, has its roots in observation and experience—direct or vicarious. *All learned behavior can be unlearned.* If undesired behavior is habitual, it takes time to unlearn it because it takes *alternative experiences whose advantages come to be recognized as outweighing the previous rewards* perceived to be gained by the behavior destined for extinction.[1]

Children's anger often comes from some manner and degree of rejection by their parents and/or close family members at an early age. Deprived of nurturance and affection, children grow up feeling powerless and helpless—causing fear, suspicion, and antagonism to underpin their view of people and the world. They are difficult to control and lack peer friendships. [2]

Many angry children are not victimizers or bullies; they continue to be the victims and bullied ones until an opportunity presents itself to act out in a dramatic way. Still other children manipulate their way through life, using others as they are used, perpetuating the cycle of abuse they endure.

Sometimes students who seem to be innately mean and cruel are referred successfully to certified professionals in anger-management programs. However, classroom teachers know that those opportunities are in short supply. The needy students whose daily behavior seems fed by anger, even rage, will likely still be in class throughout their participation in most programs. The teachers and support staff who work with them should try to understand the reasons behind such anger and what to do to minimize unsettling outbursts.

It takes a teacher with compassion, insight, personal security, and self-control to deal effectively with students whose behavior shows none of those traits. A teacher's attention to hostile students must be intentional, intelligent, and skillful. There are three keys to success and effectiveness in this area:

1. Use strategies that minimize angry feelings
2. Know how to teach prosocial skills that support anger control and management
3. Recognize that the absence of opportunity is a catalyst for anger and disconnection from learning

MINIMIZE ANGRY FEELINGS IN SCHOOL

Although it is clear that students' anger comes from many sources, disruptions and altercations in school are likely to occur when circumstances affect students' perceptions of their *safety, security, or self-image.*

Regardless of the exact situations, there are things that help all interactions with students driven by angry behavior. Kindness works. Calm must prevail. Quiet helps. Low light enhances a peaceful ambience. Patience is a must. Verbal acceptance and appreciation of expressed anger are important. Happily, teachers are given the opportunity to make a contribution every day, no matter how small, to offset the weight of sadness, confusion, and hostility so many students carry.

The following examples explore three school issues—fighting, bullying, and extortion—where *safety* becomes a factor that exacerbates anger.

Example #1 — Safety/Fighting

Joseph had an argument with Roger during lunch that turned into a fistfight.

Both boys gave in to an outward expression of their anger, risking bodily harm one to the other. The teacher conversation about the dangers of fighting, its ineffectiveness as a way to settle differences, the resulting punishment or mediation should be as brief as possible.

The interaction between the teacher and the boys, alone or together, should model collaborative behavior that has no anger in it at all:

> Ms. Gentile: *"Roger and Joe, I realize that you are angry at each other, but I want you to notice that I am not angry with you at all. Would one of you agree to let the other have the first turn, without interruption, to tell me what happened the way you see it?"*

The teacher must use as many active listening skills as possible as the stories unfold. The end result should be that the boys have had an opportunity to problem-solve a different way to settle their disagreement, with a teacher who made an honest attempt to appreciate their angry response while modeling how a peaceful demeanor looks, sounds, and feels.

Example #2 — Safety/Bullying

Mr. Kraft watched Rosalinda give her chemistry homework to Steve to copy for the third time this week. She was clearly unhappy about it and warned him to leave her brother Miguel alone. Mr. Kraft spoke to Rosalinda about his observation and asked to meet with her.

The anger that Rosalinda feels as a receiver of Steve's bullying behavior may or may not surface immediately during their meeting. Rosalinda will be on guard. Mr. Kraft should state that three times in a week he saw Rosalinda sacrifice her academic work to Steve, allowing herself to be intimidated by his overbearing attitude and threat. He should let her know he understands why she allowed fear of Steve and fear for her brother's safety to override her desire to be free of him.

In so doing, this young lady reinforced her irrational self-talk that told her she was powerless against Steve and fanned whatever angry flames she may carry with her about people, males, school, or personal weakness.

When bullying behavior comes to teachers' attention, it is usual to intervene directly and quickly. Recriminations and admonitions are dispensed plentifully to the bully, and clear orders are given that such behavior cease and desist. Enforcing actions that actually stop the bully are difficult at best.

However, Mr. Kraft was a teacher with insight into anger-management principles, and he chose to intervene in this dilemma differently. During the meeting, Mr. Kraft was surprised how well Rosalinda eventually recognized and verbalized her anger. His intervention to bring resolution involved mediation; that is, he encouraged and persuaded Rosalinda to meet face-to-face with Steve while he acted as the moderator.

Before that meeting, Mr. Kraft engaged Rosalinda in conversation that set her at ease and allowed Rosalinda *multiple times* to role-play what she would say to Steve. It may have been the first time that Rosalinda put words to her anger and fear in a reasoned way; helping her do that gave her a great gift of personal power.

Offering ongoing support and guidance to Rosalinda would surely build relationship, as issues relating to personal growth rely on both influence and trust. Rosalinda was fortunate to have found someone who recognized how to merge anger-management strategies with personal support.

Example #3—Safety/Extortion

Ron bought Jeff potato chips from the snack line because Jeff threatened that he and his friends would follow Ron home after school and cause trouble. The "lunch lady" reported the threat to Ron's homeroom teacher, Mrs. Simpson.

Ron's dislike for Jeff is active, and each time he feels forced to buy Jeff potato chips, his resentment grows into angry imaginings about how to "give him what he deserves." However, his fear of after-school repercussions is greater than his will to refuse Jeff or seek adult assistance.

More often than not, students will project unresolved anger onto their teachers, peers, or situations seemingly unrelated to any known cause for hostility. This often occurs in classrooms after lunch, where unresolved social actions simmer in students' minds. Being conscious of this enables teachers to remember that, in most instances, students' anger should not be taken personally. Although it may *feel* very personal, teachers who understand the true nature of unresolved anger can readily disassociate from the intensity of it and redirect their attention to the root causes behind its furious expression.

Mrs. Simpson, apprised by the lunch staff member about Ron's predicament, should immediately appreciate that Ron needs to address the anger and resentment he feels about Jeff's extortion. Ron may have demonstrated angry behavior in class that seemed misdirected, or maybe not. In either case, an opportunity exists to help Ron learn something about anger management that is useful now and in the future.

The wisdom and perspective gained from years of life as an adult can cause forgetfulness that students are experiencing feelings they think are unique to them. In Ron's case, as an example, the teacher can provide Ron great relief by assuring him that his angry thoughts are normal.

Mrs. Simpson: *"Ron, let's talk about the lunchroom, today. Mrs. Cartina told me what happened between you and Jeff. Let me just say that I'd really be angry if Mr. Jones forced me to buy him dessert every day just because we share this classroom."*

By choosing to show genuine interest in Ron's problem, the teacher will be inviting him to connect with someone who can offer new ways to deal with issues of anger, fear, and self-confidence. *"Here's what I think I'd say to Mr. Jones . . . What could you say to Jeff?"* Listen. Supply words and phrases to help Ron. Practice several times. Be very encouraging. Insist that he try. Assure him that Jeff is wrong, and that he can stop being victimized.

A positive personal connection as simple as this could become a helping relationship. Through Mrs. Simpson's understanding and support, Ron's thoughts about teachers, his ability to problem-solve, and his perception of personal power could begin to change.

The next examples explore three school issues—poor academic skills, social isolation, and lack of necessary school supplies, where *security* becomes a factor that exacerbates anger.

Example #1—Security/Poor Academic Skills

Natalie is a sixth-grade girl whose reading and writing skills are at the fourth-grade level. She is hostile with her peers and impatient during instruction time. She seldom completes her work and resists teacher attempts to explain ways to improve.

Natalie's teacher will have to create opportunities for academic (and social) success for Natalie, despite her current inability to do average sixth-grade work. Facilitating opportunities for success where Natalie can earn genuine praise is a good way to make Natalie more open to a positive personal connection to her teacher. Being certain of exactly *why* Natalie is so far behind will influence what types of differentiated instruction best suit Natalie's needs.

Consider all support school staff as helpers. Establish the strongest connection possible with Natalie's parents or guardians. It would help Natalie if her peers could get to know her apart from academic work. Perhaps some community-building activities could serve that purpose. Explore community resources that might be an outlet for Natalie. Finding ways to let Natalie know that her teacher values her for who she is, much more than for what she can do, is essential.

The need to belong is a universal value, prevalent in all societies and across all cultures. In the school community, students whose poor academic skills prevent them from performing required tasks with reasonable success rightly feel out of place. Failure to "fit" in the school setting, in and of itself, can cause a student to become disheartened and discouraged.

In addition, feeling like a misfit will reinforce whatever insecurities a student like Natalie already carries from life experiences, contributing to a self-fulfilling prophecy that guarantees failure on all fronts. Displays of angry behavior because of such negative feelings are common, especially in adolescence, when peer acceptance and equality are paramount needs.

Sometimes teachers fail to recognize that students' disruptive or uncooperative behavior directly relates to being unable to reach whatever standards of academic performance are the norm for the class in which they are placed. This is a particularly perplexing problem for both teachers and students, because most school systems require teachers to meet and exceed established grade-level standards.

Although that enigma remains unsolved, this is also true: Unless and until students' school experience allows them to feel some measure of reasonable success in both the academic and social arena, the feelings that accompany *not* doing so will interfere with students' personal growth and test teachers' ability to manage classroom behavior fueled by anger.

Example #2—Security/Social Isolation

Lee, a high school sophomore, is a "loner." He fits the stereotype perfectly. He rarely engages in conversation, has no known friends at school, eats alone at lunch, wears clothes that are not typical for teens his age, does not participate in class voluntarily, attends no school social functions. He seems not to notice the glances or comments of his peers, and deals dispassionately with the occasional confrontational taunts of "the boys."

Students such as Lee, who present themselves as loners, are not, by that fact, students whom teachers should automatically consider in need of intervention for aberrant behavior.

It is important for teachers to make an effort *not* to accommodate a withdrawn student's silent message—"leave me alone"—until the teacher is satisfied, based on more than an intuitive feeling, that a student such as Lee is simply a healthy introvert.

For certain then, teachers need to attempt to create a positive personal connection by reaching out to Lee in as many ways as possible. Speak to him directly every day. Ask about his interests. Follow up with references to them, magazine articles, media connections, or further questions. Ask him for help. Comment on his academic work through specific feedback, notes written separately, or conversation. Find positive reasons to call home to speak with a parent or guardian. Accept any obvious eccentricities as neutrally as possible.

In this way teachers can and should assess whether a student who is a loner might be at risk and in need of professional intervention. Withdrawal from others or from life in general is one of the hallmarks of depression. Chronic depression is a prolonged feeling of sadness, hopelessness, or withdrawal that can mark a severe form of psychopathology.[3]

Too many and too recent news reports have revealed the misery, unhappiness, anger, and rage kept in check by some students who are, or choose to be, isolated from their peers. Too often, these emotions find an explosive outlet that leaves everyone filled with remorse and regret. For a teacher, "I could have or should have known" is one of the greatest regrets of all.

Research has identified empathy and social skills as basic competencies that determine how we handle relationships.[4] Teachers who are quick to pick up signals from their students' feelings and concerns are more likely to respond to students' unspoken needs than those who do not pay attention to emotional signals or value them. In tandem with empathy, teachers who have mastered a variety of personal social skills can affect change in others more readily and can teach students social skills they may lack.

Example #3—Security/Lack of Necessary School Supplies

Sherod came to class again without pencil, paper, books, or assignment pad. He acts as if he doesn't care that instruction time is lost trying to facilitate his participation.

Juanita lost her lunch money—again. Why this keeps happening is unclear.

James said he was late because he was looking to borrow someone's cell phone. He doesn't know who will pick up his sister from elementary school today.

At first glance, it would seem that the problems of the above students have nothing at all to do with threatening their security at school. Could those problems exacerbate anger-driven behavior that may steal instruction time and challenge a teacher's anger management skills? Yes.

Mr. Taylor: *"Sherod, look inside of this box. It has paper, pencils, and assignment sheets. It's yours to keep here for when you need it. To me, the most important thing is that you come here and actually learn, not cause delays over having forgotten, lost, or whatever, your supplies. Please still try to come prepared, but for now, let's stop arguing over this every day. I'll leave this box on the bottom shelf."*

Mrs. Clauss: *"Juanita, we need to talk about why you keep losing your lunch money! I certainly don't want you to go without lunch. Help me help you. What should we do about this?"* Wait for Juanita to say something. Build on that, or, ask, *"What you are willing to do for a possible solution?"* Offer a solution of your own: *"I'm willing to work something out with the cafeteria, maybe like a ticket that turns into an IOU. But, know that I will need to talk to your mom at the end of the week to get that money. What do you think?"*

Ms. Vincent: *"James, you are carrying a big burden. Why on earth didn't you tell us you are feeling responsible for your little sister? Every problem has a solution, but we need each other sometimes to help. What do you need to happen so you can be able to concentrate on school? I can let you use the office phone for something as important as this, but not every period. Tell me more. Is there a time or place where you can contact whomever you need to be sure she is not waiting and crying? Tell me . . ."*

These students' stress, even though it is perhaps of their own making, leads them to the same place—where frustration, uncertainty, and impatience trigger whatever negative self-talk they have learned to think. These thoughts, in turn, cause them to feel and then act the way they think, resulting in an angry defense of their angry behavior. It is worth noting: "Personal frustrations are probably the most frequent triggering events that result in negative thoughts and angry feelings."[5]

Consider that these seemingly small problems show how frustration, impatience, and uncertainty, first cousins of anger, are always ready and waiting to set the stage for their favorite relative. Collectively, these feelings undermine security, a primary prerequisite for school success. A sense of safety eliminates fear, worry, and threat of danger. Students and parents have the right to expect schools to be such safe havens. The reality is frequently different from what parents and students should be guaranteed.

In order to minimize angry behavior rooted in insecurity, the most important first step a teacher can take is to pause before dismissing problems as trivial or simply annoying. In the above examples, the students' perception compromises their security. Knowing this, teachers should try to set aside their own under-reaction and/or annoyance and assume a let-me-help-you-solve-this stance.

Often, this helping attitude, or expressed appreciation of the student's dilemma, will be enough to ward off an angry outburst or disrespectful response. If the opportunity presents itself, an actual problem-solving session would be useful and likely enhance a student's belief in the teacher's role as one who cares.

The final three examples explore public criticism, teasing, and absence of opportunity, where *self-image* becomes a factor that causes or exacerbates anger:

Example #1—Self-image/Public Criticism

Many teachers have a misconception about the educational application of "correction" and "criticism." Correcting errors in students' academic work, thought processes, and behavior is an integral part of a teacher's role. It becomes second nature for teachers who try to lead, guide, model, affirm, and support students throughout the school day.

The words "correct" and "criticize" might lead some to say the application of one is synonymous with the other; that *both* words have a rightful place in the interchange between students and teachers. Careful consideration of both terms reveals essential differences in their application. To criticize, by definition, means "to find fault with someone or something; to judge the merits and faults of someone or something." Even more telling are its synonyms: blame, reprehend, censure, condemn, denounce.[6]

> Mrs. Warner: *"That's it. I've had enough of your behavior and back talk, Edward. I doubt you speak to your mother that way! I bet she's sorry she had you! Get out!"*

An example as dramatic and, unfortunately, as true as this, clearly presents the connection between anger and public criticism. Most teachers, thankfully, could say with righteous indignation, "I would *never* say something like that to a student!"

A less dramatic example shows how easily teachers can make the same point and reach the same goal by eliminating public criticism.

> Mr. Waterford (*criticism* in class): *"John, I'm returning your test. C'mon! If you can manage to write so I can read it, I'll give it a go, again."*

Correction is the "act of pointing out errors or mistakes according to a just standard, as truth, propriety or justice." Correction refers to indicating, marking, or removing errors.[7]

> Mr. Waterford (*correction* in class): *"John, I'm returning your test. Stop by and I'll explain why. I have an idea that will make your grade even better."*

Teachers who are habitual in the understanding and application of correction instead of criticism are able to invite students to consider, even welcome the growth that comes from learning from mistakes. They are teachers who are actively aware that at every age, our growth, development, and life experiences reinforce and defend our self-image, whether it is primarily positive or negative.

In times of need, crisis, or perceived threat, sorting courses of action, options, and anticipated outcomes takes place. That which most likely preserves or enhances self-image becomes a choice. For students in school, this includes not trying, so as not to fail; living up to and exceeding teachers' negative expectations; hurting others before they hurt you; and keeping anger ready to defend these positions.

In the public eye of the classroom, teachers' body language, tone of voice, facial expression, word choice, and intent accompany "correction." If students sense criticism instead of genuine, sensitive correction, then their negative self-image is reinforced; angry feelings are exacerbated and used to justify their misbehavior.

Example #2—Self-image/Teasing

Diana, crying: *"Michael and Manny pulled on my ponytail and said I wore it because I'm fat as a horse!"*

In the cafeteria: *"Hey, Nerdboy! Short one! Have you invented anything lately? Why don't you work on some tall pills?"*

In class: *"Sylvia, I'd like your attention. Shall I name the person you're thinking about? I bet I can."*

It is remarkable that teasing, with so many proven drawbacks, continues to be prevalent, overlooked, and even tolerated in schools. School shootings, murders, and suicides in the United States and foreign countries are recent and too numerous. Police, prison wardens, psychologists, and psychiatrists collect sobering facts in attempting to explain what happened. Reporters publicize them. Despite the role that teasing played in many of these events, people continue to tease others. They believe that *their* application of teasing is not the harmful kind.

The problem with teasing is that its character can change quickly from a lighthearted way to joke, flatter, gain attention and social standing to a way to bully, provoke, denigrate, and humiliate someone. Teasing assails one's self-image—the most personal part of an individual. Teasing, cynicism, and sarcasm all require complicated mental processing typical of higher-level thinking.

A significant side effect of teasing is the feeling of powerlessness that it engenders. The younger the student, the more difficult it is to exercise the emotional skill necessary to understand a tease and then to interpret its intent accurately. The cognitive ability of the majority of elementary school students is limited to concrete interpretations of the world.

Adolescents' developmental age also compounds their ability to withstand, understand, and deal positively with teasing. Adolescence is a time of establishing independence while increasing dependence upon peer relationships. Young people at this age are searching for identity and often find themselves shamed, hurt, and confused by teasing that makes them the expensive target of someone else's fun or power trip.

Michael Carneal was fourteen years old when he killed three students and wounded five in his Kentucky school. He told a court psychiatrist that he felt going to prison would be better than continuing to endure being teased about his small stature and quiet manner.[8] Without competent and sensitive adult assistance, students' self-made strategies for dealing with mean-spirited teasing causes anger that fuels get-even fantasies for some, turns inward to self-hatred for others, and prescribes unnecessary and damaging social isolation for still others.

Teachers who wish to minimize the anger fueled by a school environment that tolerates teasing should:

- Treat students' complaints about teasing seriously, resisting the temptation to rely on the tried but *not true* remedy, "Just ignore it." It is normal and healthy for students to reach out for adult support when handling a situation on their own feels insurmountable.

  Listen to the problem.

  Help the student identify what he is feeling.

  Assure the student that his feelings do not have to translate into dangerous actions.

  Use school support staff intervention if warranted.
- Create ways to bolster the self-pride of students who are chronic victims of teasing.
- Resist all teasing yourself, no matter how lighthearted or well intentioned it is.

  "Roxanne, am I your favorite teacher?"

  "Well, well, it's nice to see you in school for a change!"

  "What will you pay me for a bathroom pass?"
- Pay attention to behavior changes that can be markers for students' flight from teasing or bullying behavior:

  Sudden lateness to class

  Unusual withdrawal from social activities

  "Lost" items

  Increased hostility toward others

  Absences from school

  Academic achievement changes

- Influence the classes you teach by instructing them about the real, far-reaching effects of teasing others.

Example #3—Self-image/Absence of Opportunity

Jane is one of the overwhelming numbers of students in school systems where individual attention, proven as the key solution to so many different problems, becomes a daily and sometimes daunting challenge for teachers who realize the importance of educating minds *and* hearts. Despite the challenge, it is an essential teacher task to enable *all* students to feel counted among their peers as worthy of positive remarks from their teachers and others; they should all enjoy some measure of genuine academic success.

Mrs. Newman:

September: *"Jane, you cannot go to the science lab orientation today because your homework is incomplete. Stay here and work on it."*

October: *"Jane, there is no point in signing up for the step team, because your grades are too low. You need to work harder on your school work."*

November: *"I am so proud that ten of you made the high honor roll. Congratulations! The pizza party will be on Friday during lunch."* Jane did not qualify.

December: *"Jane, I hope you realize that your five-day school suspension put you even farther behind in your work. You need to make better choices, young lady."*

January: *"It was hard to choose the cast for the school play because so many of you tried out and did such a good job! The students in the play this year are . . ."* Jane was not selected.

February: *"Jane, we are trying to move forward here, and you are holding us back. Please stop it."*

March . . . April . . . May . . . June . . .

Most of the time, no malice is intended in teacher actions that cause a student to feel disconnected from her education experience. Nothing Jane's teacher said or did was unjustified. But Jane is likely to have translated her experience of school and her teacher's neutral stance as a reinforcement of her inner fear that she doesn't and cannot measure up to her peers or the academic tasks at hand.

Jane represents the countless students for whom the daily school experience represents the *absence of opportunity* rather than its presence. Students such as Jane are members of a group of students who move through the school system unnoticed, except for occasional, brief encounters with their teachers about academic grades or behavior.

Inferiority breeds resentment, unhappiness, and envy. Many teachers deal with hundreds of students a day. The comment, *"Jane, . . . you are holding us back"* is instantly forgotten by the teacher but not so quickly by Jane, who will use it to strengthen her case against herself and to justify an angry attitude about school, her peers, and her teachers. A less *critical* choice of words could draw Jane's attention; a private, positive conversation with Jane about her behavior would be even better.

The opportunity to receive an education rivals no other in its potential to impact one's present and future so completely. Once begun, students come to know that the time given to their school experience occupies the major part of their life, at least until the minimum goal—high school graduation—is achieved.

The assumption, on the part of parents and teachers, is that schooling enhances the cognitive, social, emotional, and moral development of each student. They expect that school will make right whatever developmental wrongs there are, as well as remedy any attitudes caused by events or influences outside of school.

Actualizing these assumptions propels billion-dollar budgets, teacher education programs, and endless school reform movements. In the end, it is excellent *teachers* who assure that education will ultimately produce the lifelong learners that the rapid pace of our society requires.

To minimize angry behavior displayed by students who seem unable to keep up with the academic and/or social pace of their peers, the truly simple solution is this:

1. *Notice* the students who are seldom in a position to receive praise for successful academic work or whose poor social skills limit their acceptance by their peers.
2. Create opportunities for them, *no matter how small*, to experience positive attention. Students are astute at discerning a teacher's acceptance or annoyance with regard to class members. When given the consistent example of how to value someone (everyone) by a teacher, classmates will learn to do likewise.

Minimizing the anger expressed so frequently by students because of perceived threats to their safety, security, and/or self-image in school clearly requires insight, effort, empathy, and determination. The benefits from applying the suggestions offered in this chapter are many, for students and teachers alike. The best news is that students' anger *can* be minimized. It can even be replaced by positive alternative experiences that, in time, alter the destructive self-talk that guarantees unhappiness.

TEACHING PRO-SOCIAL SKILLS THAT EMPOWER STUDENTS TO SELF-MANAGE

Numerous researchers and their collaborators have produced reference materials of all kinds, citing impressive data that suggest teaching pro-social skills is an optimum way to help students manage their behavior and control anger. Debates and controversy about the most effective ways to teach these skills continue to occupy the main stage of discussions between and among teachers, child-care workers, therapists, counselors, and all others who have a stake in the growth and development of children. All agree that teaching a social skill must be more than a cognitive exercise, especially for those whose negative behavior calls for intensive modification.

Telling others to do something, *explaining* why it is a good thing to do, *inviting* them to do it, *modeling* (only) the thing to be done, and/or *threatening punishment* if it is not done affects little or no lasting change on the part of the persons involved in the corrective process. There must be opportunities to *practice a skill* for the process to have any effect at all. Sometimes the process can move quickly without any consciousness of the steps. At other times, the process can be both formal and deliberate, and, consequently, quite slow.

Briefly, acquiring a new social skill always involves a four-step process, according to Arnold Goldstein, a leader in the field of reclaiming youth at risk.[9]

These are the basic steps:

1. The new skill must be *modeled* appropriately and in several ways that show its useful and universal application to real-life situations. For example, skills such as *dealing with an accusation, responding to others' feelings, and giving/receiving a compliment* hold promise for gaining positive benefits at home, in school, among peers, and/or in the neighborhood.
2. Once modeled, the person who has judged the skill as worthy of emulation *must have the opportunity to practice it* in the presence of others.
3. At this point, the most important part of the process comes into play. There must be *feedback* in the form of attention, praise, regard, admiration, comment, support, encouragement, surprise, or delight from

persons who observe the new skill being practiced. This is what tempts the person using the new skill to remember it, to feel that the benefits of using it outweigh the rewards of the opposite behavior, and to realize the power of a positive, self-determining skill. The new user must be conscious of the feedback.

4. Lastly, the new skill must be perceived to be one that will *transfer* into different aspects of daily life regularly and then habitually. This is when the new user owns the skill.

Currently, more and more teachers lament the absence of social skills that students should exercise at school. Many students present themselves without having previously learned or practiced enough basic social skills at home, in church, among relatives and friends, or within the community. In their place are behaviors that do not offer positive self-determination or empowering self-confidence.

Unfortunately, a triple task confronts teachers—teaching subject matter, helping students *unlearn* acquired antisocial attitudes and behaviors, and directing the new learning of positive social skills to replace them. The most significant obstacle that prevents teachers from teaching pro-social skills successfully is the *time* it takes to apply steps two and three of the process described above. Students cannot transfer new social skills into daily use without *practice and feedback*. Without even attempting to teach social skills, most teachers would agree that the school day is already too short.

This fact gives rise to two essential questions:

1. Can academic instruction take place successfully when students' school behavior reveals little or no habitual practice of basic social skills?

2. Is social skill acquisition important enough to warrant teachers' devoting some of the time allotted for academic instruction to the formal teaching of social skills?

Teachers will say that the answer to the first question has to be "Yes," because they are bound by the rules and regulations prescribed by course requirements, testing procedures, assessment instruments, and teacher evaluations. At the same time, teachers unanimously concede that the absence of basic social skills makes successful teaching more challenging. Behavioral issues that develop because social skills are absent undoubtedly impact instructional time.

Regarding the second question, all teachers engage in some form of social skill teaching every day. Usually, step one, modeling, is the frequent and obvious instrument of influence. As powerful as modeling is, it cannot stand alone to enable a new skill to be acquired or transfer to daily use. [10] Beyond modeling, most teachers, especially in middle and secondary school, will speak with urgency about the clear connection between academic achievement and strong social skills, yet feel powerless to find time to follow the four-step process to its completion. It is a true dilemma.

For resistant learners in need of anger-management training, unproductive habits of mind and action interfere with every day's events. Their habitual negative actions become "the tail that wags the dog." Remember, resistant students likely have no connection to the kind of optimism that assures or values successful academic performance, complements athleticism, and denotes good physical and mental health.

For them, skills for dealing with positive events, such as responding to the feelings of others, helping others, and expressing affection appropriately are essential skills. Skills for dealing with unpleasant events, such as expressing a complaint, responding to someone else's anger, dealing with an accusation, and keeping out of fights, are just some of the skills that would help mitigate the anger that directs their behavior. Such skills need to be learned sooner rather than later.

Teachers who are willing to invest time in helping students acquire social skills should:

- Learn to use the four-step process for teaching a social skill. Never eliminate the second and third steps.
- Set aside dedicated time to teach a select number of pro-social skills. Allow the dominant needs of your students guide you to the choices you make. Selecting *five skills* to teach during a school year would be an outstanding gift.
- Become familiar with the teacher resources readily available on this topic.
- Offer habitual public acknowledgment of positive social skills practiced by your students.
- Seek professional development related to aggression replacement techniques.
- Be patient.

There are schools, residential treatment centers, and juvenile detention centers that make accommodations or alterations in the academic day to allow skilled teachers to give consistent, dedicated time and effort to teaching pro-social skills. The benefit to students is an opportunity to learn how to live a new and different life that is in their power to control.

Water tames angry flames. Water extinguishes fire, and new growth follows thereafter. Water forces change. Caring teachers are life-giving water.

POINTS TO REMEMBER

- Aggression is a *learned* behavior; all learned behaviors can be unlearned.
- In school, issues related to safety, security, and self-image often exacerbate students' angry feelings. Teachers must be intentional about creating specific ways to safeguard these things in their classroom communities.
- Pro-social skills need to be modeled, practiced, reinforced by specific feedback, and shown to have several useful applications. Teaching just five social skills in this way during a school year could have a lifetime effect on the students who learn them.

NOTES

1. Goldstein, Arnold, and Barry Glick. *Aggression Replacement Training.* Champaign, IL: Research Press, 1987.

2. Magid, Ken, and Carole A. McKelvey. *High Risk: Children without a Conscience.* Golden, CO: M & M Publishing, 1987.

3. Long, Nicholas, and William C. Morse. *Conflict in the Classroom.* Austin, TX: Pro-Ed, 1996.

4. Goleman, Daniel. *Working with Emotional Intelligence.* New York: Bantam Doubleday Dell Publishing Group, 1998.

5. Long and Morse. *Conflict in the Classroom.*

6. *The American Heritage Dictionary of the English Language,* 3rd ed., s.v. "criticize."

7. Ibid.

8. Cloud/Springfield, John. "Of Arms and the Boy," *Time*, June 2001, 38.

9. Goldstein and Glick. *Aggression Replacement Training.*

10. Ibid.

Chapter 5

The Amazing Maze

Punishment, Consequences, and Responsibility

Certainly, in taking revenge, a man is but even with his enemy, but in passing it over, he is superior, for it is a prince's part to pardon. . . . There is no man doth a wrong for the wrong's sake; but thereby to purchase profit, or pleasure, or honor, or the like.
—Francis Bacon, *On Revenge*

It takes but an instant to recall a time when punishment followed a misdeed done at home or school. The admonition "Don't do that!" said in words or by actions, or both, by adults or teachers sends a clear message. Sometimes, "OK, I won't!" represents a firm intention to comply with the directive indefinitely. Sooner or later, the question arises, "Why is it necessary to obey someone else?," and seems to have no logical answer.

Often the ability, desire, or resolve to conform to the standard raised up by those in authority wavers. Efforts to attempt or actually change one's behavior only occur when the person who owns the behavior decides to do so.

Suzanne: *"The demonstration clock in our kindergarten class was four feet high, with hands that Sister Angela moved to show us minutes and hours. She told us never to touch it. I never did, after the time I knocked it over with a thunderous crash. I cried. Sister Angela made me sit at a table by myself. I decided to stay far away from that clock!"*

Steve: *"I remember well the time my dad waited up for me when I was in high school and missed my curfew by three hours. I never did that again!"*

Melinda: *"My mom told my brother and me never to use the stove unless she was in the kitchen with us. We tried making soup by ourselves one day. He was six. I was seven. It spilled and burned my brother's foot. She was very angry with us. She slapped me for disobeying."*

Jim: *"My dad was a policeman. When I was five, he took me down to the station in his patrol car, telling me that, unless I was lucky, his boss would have to put me in jail for playing with matches behind the garage. I remember being scared, but I also remember playing with matches many more times after that. I never got caught again."*

BethAnn: *"In high school, I had a teacher who spent an entire class period explaining how wrong it is to be homosexual. She told us that people who choose that lifestyle ruin their lives and that teachers who profess to be gay should lose their state certificates. She was so sure of herself. It was the first time I did not accept a teacher's opinion. My older brother is gay."*

Catherine: *"For the longest time, I tried not to bite my fingernails. My mom used to give me extra allowance for not doing it and docked me if I kept it up. My sister told me looking at my fingers made her sick. Once, I went for three months without doing it. I don't know why I went back to it. I didn't stop until I was in college."*

Memories of familiar situations such as these underscore the constant role that coercion and/or threats of punishment play in shaping perceptions of what is supposed to be good and the right thing to do.

Coercion fails to encourage or allow free choice, without which there is neither ownership nor responsibility for actions. Cooperation by coercion may lead to full conformity, partial acquiescence, or outright rejection as a response to behave in certain ways. However, it is an extrinsic controller unrelated to the intrinsic desire and motivation to change behavior. The desire and motivation belong only to the person who decides to change the behavior in question.

Punishment is a powerful teacher. It leaves many lasting impressions on its pupils: might makes right, anger and violence are justifiable partners, power gives legal license, self-incrimination is deserved—to name just some of the long-term convictions carried after experiencing punishment. Punishment rarely motivates building or maintaining a relationship with someone. The more punishment is used to affect behavior change, the more resistance to trust others increases.

PUNISHMENT AND MOTIVATION

Punishment involves making a judgment that someone's actions display a fault, offense, or violation against a standard of acceptable behavior. It involves imposing a penalty—pain, suffering, shame, strict restraint, or loss—on the person whose actions fall short of the proposed standard. Punishment can be self-imposed, or imposed by someone else. Research in the field of operant conditioning and human motivation shed some light on why punishment is such a powerful tool to use when trying to make someone who is reluctant to do so conform to a desired standard.

In his research on human behavior, B. F. Skinner proposed that consequences of actions, more than actions themselves, control behavior. Therefore, by controlling consequences, one can control behavior. Skinner's work identifies two kinds of punishment. One kind is arranged intentionally by others to induce people *not* to behave in certain ways; the other is the aversive influence of natural "punishments," such as being burned by touching a hot stove. Skinner's operant conditioning research holds credibility, because it aligns closely with actual experiences of punishment. [1]

Most significant for those who would like to influence unwanted, inappropriate, or self-destructive behaviors by using punishment is the understanding that punishment *will cause behaviors to be suppressed but not changed.* Punished behaviors, especially if the behaviors are habitual, generally return as soon as the aversive contingency is withdrawn.

Many terms describe the ways people try to evade punishment. Some *rationalize*, some *displace* the inevitable anger or resentment punishment causes, others may *identify* with the punisher, others *project* bad, punishable behavior onto others. Still others *avoid* neutral circumstances in case punishment may be attached, or *sublimate* by adopting a similar behavior less easily punishable to replace the one that brought punishment.

David McClelland, in his work on human motivation, notes that three elements interact as determinants of behavior. These elements are motivation, skill, and cognitive variables. [2]

Motivation constitutes one's efforts to achieve a goal. *Skill* determines one's ability to reach a goal. *Cognitive variables*—such as beliefs, expectations, and understandings about the outcome of achieving a desired goal—contribute to its possible successful achievement.

McClelland further identifies four major, complex motive systems—*achievement*, *power*, *affiliation*, and *avoidance*—within which both positive and negative expressions of behavior have their root. One motive system generally becomes the preferred motivator for an individual, driving both conscious and unconscious behavior.

Punishment, whether imposed from within or without, is incredibly influential when it deprives an individual of what his motivation system values as essential. Therefore, teachers who can recognize the characteristics of each motivation system have a significant advantage. They know when punishments or even well-intentioned suggestions for improvement are likely to elicit a strong negative response. They can wait for a better time to intervene in situations that will likely damage efforts to build positive relationships with students.

Achievement Motive

Individuals who are primarily motivated by *achievement* have, as their incentive, doing something better for its own sake—for the intrinsic satisfaction it brings. In school, these students are *not* motivated to please a teacher to gain approval or merit an extrinsic reward. Rather, their need to achieve tends to focus on doing well at assigned tasks and having opportunities to demonstrate personal responsibility. They seek challenge in the work they do and depend on feedback related to how they are doing.

Students motivated by achievement will often display restlessness, exaggerate their actual ability, and likely believe that any means justify a desired end. For example, teachers familiar with the achievement motive would be especially sensitive about offering comments that students would perceive undermines their personal performance. It takes time and intent to become skilled at recognizing the varied ways students reveal what is motivating to them. A keen eye and some trial and error will open wide a door of influence for teachers who invest the time to become skillful.

Having a mindset intent on modeling an optimistic manner and affirmative word choices can change simple interactions students perceive to be negative:

Punishing:

  "How disappointed I am (you must be, your parents will be) to hear about what you've done (not done)."

Positive for relationship building:

  "How do you think we can work together to improve this situation?"

Punishing:

> *"I know why you failed your math test. It's because you spend too much time on music, sports, and student council. You're not 'Superstudent,' you know."*

Positive for relationship building:

> *"It's amazing how many things you try to fit in your day. Your failed math test could be related to time management. Let's talk about it."*

Punishing:

> *"Why on earth did you pick such a difficult topic? You have way too much information here."*

Positive for relationship building:

> *"Wow! You picked a challenging topic! I see some good work here. Sometimes, too much information gets in the way."*

Power Motive

Individuals primarily motivated by *power* have, as their incentive, the use of assertiveness or aggression to gain control over their circumstances, others, or perceived opportunities for advancement and/or recognition. Interestingly, the first connotation of the words "assertive" and "aggressive" is often negative, associated with an antisocial attitude or action. McClelland refers to results from a self-assessment checklist given to a sample of men and women considered possessing a strong power motive. Even they assigned negative traits to themselves first:

> There were many opportunities to pick positive adjectives like *active, adaptable, adventurous, cooperative or courageous,* which could signify an assertive disposition. It is as if the individuals high in power recognize their aggressive impulses and judge them negatively, just as society would judge them; and have a rather negative self-image in consequence. (p. 281)

In the same way, teachers are quick to see the negative aspects of the motivation needs of power students first, feeling the need to "nip in the bud" any aggressive and/or assertive behaviors, lest these students "get the upper hand" and become "troublemakers." Unfortunately, because power students present themselves so forcefully, they often fail to receive support and guidance that would help them capitalize on the positive aspects of their dominant trait.

For example, students who have a genuine need for recognition, respect, and loyalty from others will surround themselves with peers who can be led. In a classroom, student leaders who perceive their teacher as weak will vie with him or her for class control by creating power struggles at every turn. The ability of these students to develop emerging leadership skills is marked by limited opportunities and experiences. Learning to develop this trait positively is a complex process that truly needs adult support.

Punishing:

> *"John, that's enough! You seem to disagree for the sake of disagreeing. Perhaps you should come right up here and take over teaching, since you like being the center of attention so much."*

Positive for relationship building (sincerely, in a private conversation):

> *"John, I want to say that I notice some real leadership qualities in you. You seem to see both sides of an issue quickly. I'm trying to think of some ways to help your classmates see you as a leader during class. Let's talk about this for a minute."*

Punishing:

> *"Some students in here know how to cooperate instead of bossing everyone around, but that doesn't mean you, does it, Jodi? Sit down over there, young lady, and try to be quiet and listen to the directions!"*

Positive for relationship building (with kindness and a light heart, in a private meeting):

> *"Jodi, you look so nice today. I asked you to come because I want to help you learn how to ask someone if you can join a group. There are many ways to do it. Some are quite a bit better than others. Let's try some different ones. We'll see which one you like best. Here—pretend you want to join my group. What might you say?"*

Affiliation Motive

Individuals who are primarily motivated by affiliation have as their incentive concern about relationships with others. They need and seek others' approval, place value on true friendship, and work harder and better when in circumstances where warmth, empathy, and personal care are present. They are interested in people—what they say and do, how they live, and what they think and feel. For example, George Washington would be more memorable to them because he had wooden false teeth than because he was the first president of the United States.

Students who demonstrate the negative side of these traits are well known and easily recognizable to their teachers. Their fear of rejection is so strong as to make some of these students become anxious, tentative, and in need of inordinate reassurance. They are the seekers of constant praise, relentless in their demand for attention and content to get it in any way possible.

Children and adolescents who manifest a preference for the affiliation motive are in a continuous struggle as they develop. The challenge for teachers is to capitalize on the positive traits of this system and minimize the traits that are demanding, egocentric, and unpleasant. This is a delicate dance, especially because the needs of this group make them particularly vulnerable to bullying, rejection, public judgment, and thoughtless criticism.

To students for whom affiliation is a high priority, comments from teachers carry inordinate importance:

Punishing:

> "You know what? I don't really care why your homework is late again. Hello! This is the third time this week! You know the rule. It's another zero."

Positive for relationship building:

> "Thank you for explaining your reasons for the late homework. I am sorry you are having such a bad week. Since this is the third time, and you know the rule, what do you think I should do? Let's think out loud about this together."

Punishing:

> "Stop asking me, 'Is this right?' Do not get up again! I'll come to your desk when I can! I'm only one person, you know."

Positive for relationship building:

> "Oh, my goodness, here you are again! You know what I'm going to say, right? Please go to your desk and try to be patient. I'll get to you soon. Promise. Thank you."

Punishing:

> *"No, I am not in a bad mood! No, you cannot pass out the papers. How about this? You can try being quiet and doing your seatwork. Please!"*

Positive for relationship building:

> *"Do I seem to be in a bad mood? I'm probably just tired or distracted. You could help me a lot by just starting your seatwork. I really will appreciate it. Will you do that for me?"*

Having a positive personal connection to their teacher (and their peers) is *critical* for these students. Thoughtless comments from peers and adults can shift their natural bent toward becoming people who are caring, helpful, unselfish, and supportive of others to becoming dependent self-seekers, unable to act for fear of what others might say or do.

Avoidance Motive

The last motivation system McClelland identifies is avoidance. He points out that this area has received the least scientific measurement to date because it is so all-encompassing. Reducing anxiety through avoidance is a master motive for animals and humans. The different ways of reducing perceived discomfort of any kind are quite subjective and thus countless in number.

Avoidance as a motivation system is useful to consider, especially because *avoiding punishment* plays a primary role in the lives of students governed by anxiety. Evading whatever circumstances they perceive as threatening and anxiety-causing is their primary goal. Additional and/or external punishments contribute nothing to relieve their habitual anxiety. Daily school experiences are challenging, as fear of failure and/or success, fear of rejection, fear of power and/or weakness all underpin students' social and cognitive efforts.

Elementary-aged and adolescent students who are avoidant behave in very different ways. Their level of development and which fears underlie their anxiety govern the learning behavior of this group of students. Being certain of exactly what motivates these students is neither easy nor completely necessary in the school setting.

More important is knowing that punishment as a tool for behavior control does not alleviate the anxiety that already paralyzes the behavior of students who present themselves as anxious, evading, duplicitous, or hesitant. Yet, a visit to any school on any given day will reveal punishing words or actions used thoughtlessly. The hope of finding immediate solutions to behaviors that challenge the daily routine *will not be fulfilled by punishment*. Students are quick to observe that punishment is a weak teacher's tool. All but the most fearful find ways to circumvent the empty threat punishments carry.

In too many cases, students' lives outside of school are so punitive that it makes it virtually impossible for teachers to punish misdeeds in any meaningful way. Students will often say "I don't care!" in response to a teacher's threat of punishment. When teachers realize students really mean it, the loss of leverage a teacher feels is keen. The use of punishment with students whose needs are met by avoidance offers no bridge to forming a relationship that might challenge their self-talk and change their perspective.

In the following example, a well-intentioned teacher offers punishing praise to Sharon, a shy, withdrawn, unpopular girl:

Punishing:

> *"Sharon, you are the best math student in this trig class, without a doubt. Come up to the board and show the class how well you solved this problem."*

Given Sharon's usual demeanor, the teacher should consider that:

- Calling Sharon "the best math student" places a burden on her to be "the best," through the entire course, augmenting her fear of success.
- Such praise might exacerbate her unpopularity.
- Placing her in the public eye without notice or support, when she clearly avoids it, fails to appreciate the reality of her perspective.

Positive for relationship building (at Sharon's desk, not in front of the class):

> *"Sharon, this is an excellent solution to a difficult problem! Well done! Would you be willing to write it on the board? No? May I write it on the board and say you did it?"*

- Specific praise that focuses on the deed, as opposed to praise that focuses on the person, poses no burden.
- Small as it may be, this attitude honors Sharon's present view of the world and her place in it.
- Showing Sharon this level of sensitivity and respect shows her a teacher who is responsive to her needs.

Some students, avoiding the reality of their low skills or the embarrassment of its revelation to their peers, assume the role of class clown.

Punishing:

> *"Since you think everything is so funny, James, see if you think this is funny. You will not be going on the school trip to the amusement park. The requirement for 'no referrals' for bad behavior does not apply to you as of right now. Take this to the office."*

Although taking such a stance is tempting and offers some relief to a frustrated teacher, consider the effect of such punishment:

- It is short-lived relief. Now James has nothing to lose.
- It supports no change in behavior that addresses James's low skills or his fears of failure, power, or rejection.
- It causes resentment, disappointment, and hostility.
- It is public criticism that is not constructive.

Positive for relationship building:

> *"James, I've kept you after class because I need to say that I am feeling dangerously frustrated about your clowning in class. I know we've talked about this before, but here we are again. Today I almost wrote the referral that would prevent you from going to the amusement park next month. I know that particular punishment would not help anything, but I'm unsure what will make you realize that you are keeping the kids who sit around you from learning. Equally bad, your behavior is telling me that you have given up trying to learn. I do understand that it's easy to say the material is unimportant when you don't know it. It's easy not to like it. But I'm here to tell you that it is never too late to learn and that I think you can learn. So, what shall we do? Want some ideas? I want to be clear, James. The funny stuff has got to stop."* (Insist on some kind of mutual agreement. Write it down. Sign it together. Follow up.)

- A conversation such as this uses authority without undue authoritativeness.
- The teacher has made an honest attempt (again) to let James know that his fears are transparent and have hopeful outcomes in the teacher's view.
- James knows the teacher is in control of his or her emotions and willing to offer some support in exchange for his cooperation.

It bears repeating that when individuals are deprived of what their motivation system values as essential, even if the system is built on false premises or irrational beliefs, both their conscious and unconscious behavior will strive to accommodate their perceived needs.

Punishment fails to support actions driven by the need to achieve, the need to affiliate, the need to feel power, or the need to avoid something. Whenever teachers endeavor to *make positive personal connections* with students, it improves the potential outcome of whatever behavior goals are desirable.

CONSEQUENCES ARE NATURAL EFFECTS

Which of these two statements reflects an understanding of the meaning of the word "consequence"?

"In my classroom, everyone knows what the consequences are for misbehaving."

"Because your grade-point average is below 3.0, you will not be eligible for team tryouts this semester. I am sorry for your disappointment."

Undoubtedly, two component parts of the second statement make it better than the first statement. The first part makes it clear that the responsibility for ineligibility rests with the student. It then offers a genuine expression of understanding and consolation from the teacher.

Consequence is "the relation of a result to its cause; an effect" and "something that naturally follows from an action or condition."[3] One can expect that water will flow from a faucet in good repair. Rain will wet what is not under cover. An open door will chill the house on a winter's day.

Ben steals a calculator from a classmate. The consequent effect of that action is this: Ben has a calculator. Brenna leads a group of girls who destroy Marren's reputation through Internet slander. The consequent effect of that action is this: Brenna has satisfactorily hurt Marren for reasons only she knows. Strict adherence to the definition of consequence and the thoughtful consideration of it can reestablish its correct application in behavior modification and behavior management plans.

The meaning of consequence practiced in parenting and education generally refers to a designed result connected to an action by someone with power to enforce that result.

More often than not, adults who tell children that there are consequences for their actions are really reminding them that there are punishments awaiting should they choose not to comply with the norms established for good conduct.

Designing an enforceable result connected to an action is neither good nor bad, in and of itself. It is not, however, true to say, "Because you did not do X as I asked, the consequence for that is Y." It bears repeating: Consequences follow *naturally* from an action or condition. Punishments for failing to comply with a directive are not true consequences.

Whether at home or in school, adults in authority can and do create behavior management plans for things such as order, safety, schedules, family or classroom standards for behavior, maintaining value systems, and more.

When adults design enforceable results for noncompliance of family or school rules, it is important for those affected by the possible results to be forewarned so that they can exercise their right to choose to avoid an undesirable outcome.

Teachers who correctly distinguish between genuine consequences and punishments can discover positive connection opportunities that also empower students to manage their own behavior better. These opportunities focus on the freedom of choice so important to everyone. Free will is our birthright, inherent in our human nature, making us distinct from all other living things.

Both parents and teachers have the joyful role of helping children learn to balance wants with needs and to make "right" or moral choices consonant with the good of community. Learning to make such choices often happens by learning from first having made the wrong choices. Experience continues to be the very best teacher. Home and school are the optimal places for children to receive the gift of hope, the gifts of many chances, patient caring, and unconditional love.

Recall the teacher conversation from the example earlier in the chapter. The teacher who tells a student that he or she is ineligible for team tryouts can be kind, genuinely regretful, hopeful for the future and encouraging, because what happened reflects a true consequence.

The student made choices, whether or not he or she realized it, that caused his or her academic grade to be lower than allowed in order to participate in an extracurricular activity. Guidance can help the student see that the ultimate fault was, in fact, the student's. The caring process that offers guidance opens the door for ongoing direction because it is free of punishment that would likely feel personal or arbitrary.

Teachers who say, *"In my classroom, everyone knows what the consequences are for misbehaving"* have reason to be pleased that they have successfully established rules for the good of the order with results prepared for students who disobey the rules. However, students everywhere quickly understand that when teachers say, "These are the consequences," they really mean, "These are the punishments" for rule infractions. Hopefully, the results the teachers have designed are related as closely as possible to the rule infraction, will be given respectfully, and are not excessively punishing.

Generally, forewarning students that they have a choice about whether to comply with classroom rules does not happen. Students' attention is rarely directed to an equal or greater number of specific benefits to them for full compliance with classroom rules. It is here that an amazing and simple change can occur. Consequences that students perceive as punishments can become consequences that are not punishments at all. Rather, positive consequences can encourage self-esteem, self-management, and even create openings for relationship building.

Set up classroom rules so that students understand that the choice to comply with the rules of the classroom is theirs to make. Provide, in writing, complete and specific information about what outcomes they can expect for every cooperative or noncooperative choice they make.

This requires teachers to do two things that are very different from the norm:

1. Exercise initial creativity to *itemize both positive and negative outcomes* for choices
2. Resolve to *be consistent* in the application of both

To design a discipline policy that builds relationships and creates a classroom community is to take advantage of the fact that all choices are made in large part because of a perception that the choice will be advantageous in some way. Children and adolescents, especially, are just beginning to differentiate between intrinsic and extrinsic outcomes for their actions.

In order to grow educationally, socially, and emotionally, students need to be in an environment where a concerned teacher sets firm, consistent, and positive rules for behavior in a warm and supportive way. Compliance with classroom rules is necessary for the good of every student in class.

For example, teachers would be delighted to say that their students understood and obeyed these five rules:

1. Be punctual
2. Be prepared
3. Be polite
4. Pay attention
5. Participate

For the sake of this example, suppose that on the first day of school, teachers also presented the outcomes that students could expect based on the free choices they made regarding breaking or keeping the rules:

Positive Outcomes for Compliance

1. Freedom from punishment
2. Improved grades
3. Positive phone call home

4. Extra help
5. Free reading time
6. Library pass
7. Student-of-the-week nomination
8. Honor roll chance
9. Growth in knowledge
10. Positive teacher attention
11. Happy visit to principal
12. Respect of peers
13. Feeling of accomplishment
14. Teacher's sincere appreciation
15. Select prize from assorted school supplies
16. Pleasure and pride of your parents
17. Lunch with teacher
18. Use of classroom art materials
19. Free ice cream ticket
20. Words of praise photo op

Negative Outcomes for Noncompliance

1. Student/Teacher conference after school
2. Student Action Plan/Contract signed by parents
3. Loss of privileges (e.g., ineligibility for sports)
4. Home contact (phone, letter, visit)
5. Detention
6. Out-of-class referral
7. Home suspension
8. Long-term suspension
9. Poor/failing grades
10. Unhappiness

Both columns should include items that are intrinsic and extrinsic in nature. There should always be more positive outcomes for compliance than punishments for noncompliance. All *extrinsic* outcomes in either the positive or negative category should represent realistic actions for which the teacher is able and willing to accept personal responsibility.

Consistent follow-through on noticing students' compliance and pointing out the promised results to them, whether intrinsic in nature (feeling accomplished for work well done) or extrinsic in nature (positive phone call home), is absolutely necessary. Initially, adopting this plan is challenging, because most classroom management plans are reactive to inappropriate behavior almost exclusively, meting out punishment after punishment in an effort to gain control and affirm authority. Extrinsic rewards offered as bribes increase students' demands for more and better prizes. Meanwhile, a classroom community of caring students, led by a teacher who is positive and optimistic every day, slips away.

The key to relationship building here lies in the wonderful opportunity that this method offers teachers. All outcomes connected to classroom behavior now relate to lessons about choice and self-determination. In the cases of misbehavior, the onus of punishment is removed. Whether the outcomes are positive or negative, the teacher has endless chances to prompt, guide, question, commend, encourage, or commiserate with students about *the choices they make.*

Offering sincere concern and guidance when speaking to students about the outcomes *they chose* feels very different to them; the entire tone of the conversation personifies the teacher as a helper, supporter, and guide. Adopting an attitude that thinks of consequences as natural results of free choice leads children toward responsible decision making. The inevitable relationships that emerge from this attitude are not just a side benefit; they definitely make the classroom a better place. Indeed, the world would be a better place if personal responsibility for actions became common practice.

RESPONSIBILITY IS A FIVE-LETTER WORD

Brows creased, dark eyes flashing, thin arms folded over her chest, Kayla spat out the words angrily, with disdain: "You teachers! You're always tellin' us, always preachin'. Don't do this. Don't do that. Do good in school. Don't get pregnant. I know all that stuff. I already got a baby. She's six years old! My baby is my sister. I took care of that girl since my mother brought her in the door. I was the one who fed her. I changed her. I rocked her in the night. She still sleeps with me in my bed. I stole from the store to get her food. I take her shopping. I take her to school now. I talk to her teachers. Look at my school records. You'll see. I was in fifth grade. You'll see what happened to my grades. I ain't cared about school since then. I worried all the time that my mother wouldn't wake up to feed her. I begged to use the office phone. I'd run all the way home, thinking she might be dead. I stayed home from school. That girl belongs to me. She's had no momma but me since she was born! Now all of a sudden, my momma says I'm not her momma and I should get down to business at school cuz I got to graduate? Right."

Kayla learned a lot about the responsibility involved in raising a child at an early age from that best teacher, experience. In the absence of direct modeling from her mother, Kayla managed to use whatever knowledge about baby care she had and put it into practice to meet her baby sister's needs. Kayla's dramatic story underscores three key points related to acquiring personal responsibility:

1. Knowledge about responsibility becomes most useful when opportunity for practice exists.
2. Problem solving and decision making are integral parts of responsibility.
3. To be able and capable of being responsible requires self-trust and the trust of others.

Responsibility is an action. Its deeds make it known. Responsibility is a favorite buzzword in educational jargon. Teachers know that responsibility is an abstract quality like love, friendship, or loyalty. Unfortunately, its absence is lamented more than its presence is honored:

"Susan, I am tired of your irresponsible behavior!"

"Daniel, it's your responsibility to make up missed work."

"Who's responsible for this mess?"

"I begin teaching when the bell rings. It's your responsibility to get here."

"It's true! Six out of twenty-three of you handed in homework today. No kidding. You are the most irresponsible class I've had yet!"

Teachers know what responsibility is. They know they would like students to possess this most desirable trait. They wait and wish for students to acquire it. However, *responsible actions result from the actual practice of responsibility.*

Why, then, is responsibility so elusive? The answer lies in recognizing the difference between having opportunities to practice responsibility and actually practicing it, so as to experience the self-reliance it yields and the self-esteem it holds. When students learn to "take responsibility," it is a giant step toward accepting accountability. No matter what age, students need continual help and support to learn from *successful and failed* opportunities to practice being accountable.

Behavior management, part of every teacher and student's day, is one of the very best ways for teachers to help students become aware that responsibility is an action. Instead of applying and enforcing punishment only as correction for mistakes or even outright defiance, conversations between students and teachers about choice and self-determination should occur automatically. These conversations offer guidance that can lead students to begin to recognize what rationale they use to justify their behavior, what values they hold dear, what goals to set, and how to go about achieving them.

These exchanges even have power to benefit teachers in a personal way. In the process of learning how their students perceive situations, teachers become more aware of how to resist imposing their opinions and judgments about what is right and proper. Rather than making students' opinions be mirror images of their own, they allow students to hear their own voice, draw their own conclusions, and consider options for change.

Teachers who strive to help students accept personal responsibility for their actions are:

- Teachers who model responsible behavior consistently and mention the word in context whenever possible.

  "My responsibility to you is to return these papers on time. Here they are."

  "I took on the responsibility of staying after to give extra help on Mondays. I'll be here after school until . . . I hope you will come."

  "I'm responsible for hall duty right now, but I'll talk with you after class for a few minutes, if that works for you, OK?"

  "I apologize to those of you who were waiting to get into the room this morning. It's my responsibility to be here on time, but I was late today."

- Teachers who recognize that blaming others mainly attempts to shift accountability for personal behavior to someone else. Many students use it as self-protection from having to deal with the internal motives that caused their problem.

  Student: *"I only got in trouble because I got tired of waiting for you to come and help me."*

  Teacher, smiling: *"Are you telling me that whenever a student gets tired of waiting, causing trouble is the only thing he can do?"*

  Student: *"Yeah."*

  Teacher, pleasantly: *"Right. C'mon—do you think this is a reason for your behavior or an excuse? Seriously."*

(No matter what the answer, the teacher has opened the door to discussing something worthwhile.)

Notice that in one sentence, the teacher reframed the student's comment by making it a neutral query, displayed no offense regarding the accusation, and reversed the responsibility for choice back to the student.

In some cases, the blame that students present seems to represent a compelling, if not reasonable, excuse.

Student: *"I stole the money because my mother said we couldn't get groceries. I was trying to help."*

In "trying to help," this student made a choice that involved theft. Even though it was a choice made because the student could think of no other, it was an irresponsible choice. The trouble and unhappiness that accompany getting caught are natural companions to such choices. Importantly, helping teachers must keep in mind that the end does not justify the means. Students who do the wrong thing for a right reason, perhaps because they lack knowledge or willpower or other known options, should not tempt teachers to offer sympathy connected to false premises.

Some teachers rescue students from the consequences of their poor choices by allowing too many "chances." Three examples follow that show missed opportunities to help students suffer the natural consequences of their behavior:

In sports:

Coach: *"You've missed three practices and came late twice, Paul. You know the team rules. I'll let you play in tomorrow's game, but after that . . ."*

During story time:

Teacher: *"Raise your hand if you can tell me why you think Br'er Rabbit . . ."*

Sam: *"He wanted to be first!"*

Teacher: *"We raise our hand to be called on. Right, Sam?. . . Why did Br'er Rabbit . . ."*

Sam: *"He was the fastest!"*

Teacher: *"We had this problem yesterday, Sam. Now, stop interrupting."*

For out-of-class specials:

> Teacher: *"Sara, our librarian tells me that you keep your group from working there because you talk and fool around. This is the third time she has complained to me. You can have one more chance."*

Too many chances steal responsible behavior. Too many chances assure students that they are, and should be, exceptions to rules. That feeling of entitlement guarantees negative interactions with teachers and peers.

Incorporating problem-solving skills and decision making into daily classroom routines helps students experience the benefits of responsibility. Practicing responsibility is the bedrock of responsible behavior.

Three examples follow:

Example #1

> Student: *"I didn't do my homework."*

> Teacher: *"What will you do about it? You need to create a plan and tell me about your decision as soon as possible, but no later than the end of the day."*

> Student: *"I don't have my textbook, either."*

> Teacher: *"Please take a minute to think of two things you can do to solve this problem. We will be using our textbooks in class today. I'll get right back to you."* (Do not accept *"I dunno."*)

Example #2

> Student: *"You're always picking on me! I'm not the only one talking."*

> Teacher, pausing, projecting a manner that displays serious attention to student: *"I'll think about what you've just said. Can we move on right now? But I hope you have some ideas about how we can solve your concern. I'd like to talk about them after class or after school. I don't want to be thought of as having favorites. Really."*

Following through on this as immediately as possible is important, as is exploring what the student's responsibility is regarding talking during teaching time.

Example #3

> Student: *"I don't know what to write about."*

Teacher: *"The nice thing is you can choose! You might have too many thoughts at once. Write down three things you like. Then decide why someone else might enjoy knowing about it. This is a problem I know you can solve."*

Use many words, phrases, and sentences that comprise the language of problem solving, decision making, and self-determination during the teaching day. Think. Decide. Create a plan. What else can you do? Solve. Ask why? What if? Revise. Redesign. You can do this. You can fix this. Great mistake—learn from it. What did you do to improve? Each time a teacher encourages one of these notions and welcomes whatever response comes, the door to communication is open and invites students to be empowered.

The quest for student responsibility need not be complicated or daunting. Like punishment and consequences, responsibility plays an important role in bringing teachers and students to a deeper interpersonal understanding. Implied in the positive interpretation of responsibility is trust—trust that students are able and capable of being reliable in their learning and personal growth. Trust *is* a five-letter word that spells responsibility.

Navigating the maze of punishment, consequences, and responsibility is a constant challenge for those who would like to be optimistic guides in the lives of students. Every twist and turn provides an opportunity to reflect on interactions, to reframe efforts to help, and to redirect convictions while remembering that relationships matter. They are what make the journey memorable and meaningful, even life changing for both students and teachers.

POINTS TO REMEMBER

- Genuine behavior change can only occur when the person who owns the behavior decides to change it. It is an intrinsic act.
- Student motivation is connected to student ability, personal beliefs, and expectations. Teachers who are skillful motivators know what motive system likely drives the conscious and unconscious behavior of individual students.
- Punishments for failing to comply with a directive are *not* consequences.
- Choice and self-determination should be the foundations upon which all outcomes related to classroom behavior are built.
- Students need continual help and support to learn from *successful and failed* opportunities to practice being accountable.

NOTES

1. Skinner, B. F. *Beyond Freedom and Dignity.* New York: Alfred A. Knopf. 1971.
2. McClelland, David C. *Human Motivation.* Cambridge, UK: Cambridge University Press, 2000.
3. *The American Heritage Dictionary of the English Language*, 3rd ed., s.v. "consequence."

Chapter 6

Would You Read this Chapter for a Reward?

The reward of a thing well done is to have done it.
—*Ralph Waldo Emerson (1802–1882)*

Learn for the sake of learning! Learn because it gives life to the soul! Learn because it is fun! Learn because it is a privileged opportunity! Each of these maxims expresses the fond hope that education serves a greater purpose than personal advantage. It would seem that motivation to learn should be sustained by such lofty goals. However, the time, effort, and energy learning requires puts every student's motivation to the test.

What is the best way to help students acquire and maintain motivation to learn? The answer to that question is elusive. Intrinsic motivation to learn is recognized as the ideal because it indicates freedom from dependence upon external controls, such as rewards or punishments. It means that intrinsically motivated students have had life experiences that promoted their natural curiosity and interests. They are likely to have had the unwavering support of their parents or guardians. Before coming to school and through their school experience, they continue to find personal value in learning and self-management.

Extrinsic motivation factors, however, have a coveted place in society, home, and school because they offer tangible and immediate rewards for accomplishing a goal. For example, some businesses offer bonuses to employees who exceed targeted sales. Parents may reward their child for cleaning his or her room by an appointed time. Schools bestow perfect attendance awards.

It is important to state that extrinsic rewards do not directly relate to the goal itself; they neither change the effort required to reach the goal nor the time or energy it takes to reach it.

REINFORCEMENT REVISITED

When personal behavior choices lead to personally desired positive or negative outcomes, it is natural to repeat the actions that lead to those outcomes. Behaviorists since B. F. Skinner have advanced and supported the basic tenets of operant conditioning—consequences that result from behaviors greatly influence the choice of those behaviors in the first place. A pleasant or punishing consequence is a reinforcer. As such, reinforcers become powerful tools that control behavior.

In most classrooms, teachers use positive reinforcement, negative reinforcement, and punishment to control behavior. Chapter 5 noted that punishment, a short-term remedy, may suppress unwanted behavior but *does not change it*. Punishment has mainly negative effects, particularly on resistant students.

In its broadest sense, *positive reinforcement* means getting something desired. For example, a student is surprised and happy to hear that his or her teacher called home to report that improved effort resulted in greatly improved grades during the marking period. Positive reinforcement in this case has strengthened the student's behavior by making studying to improve grades desirable.

Teachers also trade extrinsic rewards, such as stars, stickers, grades, and candy, for behaviors that comply with their established classroom rules. Often, teachers use extrinsic rewards to enhance students' motivation to learn, to study, and/or otherwise fulfill their obligations as student learners. The drawback for that method, however, is that students readily make the reward their goal instead of their accomplishment.

The term *negative reinforcement* misleads many to think it represents punishment. Strictly speaking, it does not. Negative reinforcement also strengthens positive behavior. Like the receiver of positive reinforcement, the receiver of negative reinforcement feels good because it avoids or stops an undesired outcome. For example, someone may choose action X to avoid consequence Y. When action X stops or avoids consequence Y, behavior X will be repeated, or strengthened each time it is selected.

Another example: A student who suffers great anxiety related to being called upon randomly in class would feel greatly rewarded and relieved if the teacher allowed the student to signal in some way when ready to speak. Avoiding that anxiety will cause the student to be ready with dependable answers. Note that a teacher cannot help a student feel good for avoiding an undesired consequence unless the teacher first knows what consequence the student would perceive as undesired.

Holding the threat of punishment over a student and then removing it is not an application of this type of reinforcement. For example, "I will call your father immediately after class unless you change your behavior right now!" is only a threat and nothing more.

Three kinds of rewards apply to positive and negative reinforcement. There are definite drawbacks inherent in material and social rewards, cautioning the careful use of them:

1. *Material rewards* are used the most. Many teachers' desk drawers or cupboard shelves are treasure troves! Here prizes, candy, stickers, markers, charts, award certificates, or school supplies await a chance to transform someone's unacceptable behavior, if only for a moment. Material rewards present this drawback—earning a reward becomes the primary motivator. Learning itself becomes a necessary task, an obstacle even, in the way of the desired reward.

2. *Social rewards*, such as personal praise, public acclaim, Happy Visits to the principal, winks, thumbs up, or other nonmaterial signs of approval, also rank high as reinforcers. The influence of social rewards increases or decreases depending on whether the receiver holds the reward giver in high or low regard. Certain learning preferences place little or no value on material rewards. Students who receive them may offend the giver by appearing indifferent or ungrateful. Keep this drawback in mind: The experiences and self-talk of many resistant learners make them slow to trust their teachers, the school system, their peers, and themselves. Given the absence of trust, the value of social rewards as reinforcers is limited for them.

3. *Self-reward* is used the least. This is unfortunate, because it directly contributes to the growth of intrinsic motivation. For example, an astute teacher will minimize his or her praise to a student for a job well done. Instead of praise, the teacher will award that student with time and attention. This positive personal exchange will ask the student to think about and say what he did to reach a goal or to produce such fine work. Notice how this small action shifts a student's dependence on the social reward from the teacher's praise to growing self-esteem.

POSITIVE REINFORCEMENT SHOULD SAFEGUARD SELF-MANAGEMENT

Despite its long life, the debate among scholars about the principles of behaviorism continues to refine research in the field. Each decade, new information arises that questions the effectiveness of behaviorism as a premier model for explaining how reinforcement governs the learning, behaviors, and actions of human beings.

For example, Alfie Kohn's research identifies the deep roots from which today's "pop behaviorism" has emerged. He laments how the "do this and you'll get that" technique is readily accepted and practiced, within and across all levels of society. Kohn's research presents persuasive evidence that rewards and punishment fail to promote lasting behavior change, enhance performance, or recognize the importance of self-determination. [1]

Edward Deci's research in the arena of human motivation investigates the results of rewards on academic performance. He is unequivocal in his conclusions that controlling behavior by rewards undermines intrinsic motivation in every instance where it supersedes self-determination and self-motivation as a goal. [2]

Nonetheless, the reward and punishment system in schools continues to be deeply entrenched. It is part of behavior management plans, achievement motivation, athletic accomplishment, test score results, textbook examples, and grading systems. Some school districts find it difficult to imagine supporting autonomy *and* setting necessary behavior limits without relying on reward and punishment systems. A true classroom community surprises students and teachers alike when encouragement and proactive interaction replace reliance on threats, coercion, demands, and rewards.

Practicing teachers argue that, of necessity, they must live "in the moment" during the school day. Recent or long-passed classes on behavior management strategies, child psychology insights, and staff seminars on current child development markers may not be in place by memory or practice at a moment's notice. When long-term values seem out of reach, allowing and excusing reliance on extrinsic motivators for a short-term fix seems reasonable. Controlling classroom behavior becomes an end justified by whatever works. This is a slippery slope.

The two examples that follow show how quickly a reward, or promise of one, has made a bad situation worse.

Example #1

Bribes have an immediate effect—but the shortest influence—on students' behavior, and the damage they cause takes the longest to repair.

The small class of eighth graders, each with special learning needs, was glad to have someone new as part of their school day. Steve was a student teacher. Two weeks into his placement, he met with his college supervisor and declared that the students in this class were unteachable.

Ms. Hogue: *"Why? What is happening?"*

Steve, animated: *"Nothing is happening, that's what! I don't think they like me! They will not cooperate. They only work for their teacher. I have bent over backwards to help them! I have done everything to win them over. On Mondays I brought doughnuts. On Tuesdays I gave them extra free time after gym so they would settle down. I showed them YouTube movies and even brought popcorn! They appreciate nothing. All they want is more and more. It's expensive. I've called their parents, but nothing has changed."*

Mrs. Hogue: *"Steve, let's talk about all of this. First, let's review our class discussions about positive reinforcement. Then we'll address whether students like you or not."*

Example #2

Reward systems generally fail to be effective, especially when trying to control students' misbehaviors. Failure to achieve necessary control of a class or an unruly student creates desperation so keen that defeated teachers become blind to how disconnected (and dishonest, even) they become to having the means lead to a logical and worthy end.

A veteran teacher of eight years, Mrs. Bush was still a weak classroom manager, and this year's class was more rambunctious than any in her experience. Continual misbehavior diminished instruction, and pressure about the state test scores was high.

Mrs. Bush, above the noise: *"Listen up! You need to copy these notes right now! Whoever gets them finished can bring them to my desk and I will raise your science grade by one plus or minus. If you don't do it, I will lower your science grade even more by reducing it one plus or minus!"*

Clearly, Mrs. Bush's decision to raise or lower grades based on students' willingness to copy notes was unrelated to actual academic achievement.

Because schools continue to try to promote positive values and skills among students by using rewards of all kinds, coming to terms with an effective application of them is of utmost importance.

Bribes vs. Rewards that Promote Self-esteem and Self-management

Rewards that are bribes offer something to a person to influence that person's views or conduct. In classrooms, bribes become fast-acting motivators given to students to encourage learning, increase cooperation, feel successful, and force self-modification. Such positive goals make bribery appear to be quite saintly. No matter how well intentioned, *if a reward causes the receiver to act or not act in order to get the reward, it is a bribe and diminishes or replaces free choice.* Bribes quickly become the reason for performing an action. In this way, they become a replacement for *choosing to act* in a particular way or do a particular thing.

Bribes undermine freedom of choice by making offers so appealing that students can't refuse:
Bribe to her kindergarten class:

> Mrs. Silverman: *"Boys and girls, whoever is quiet during circle time will get a turn to sit on our new beanbag chair in the story corner."*

Reward that fosters self-management:

> Mrs. Silverman: *"Boys and girls, look at the story corner. We have a new beanbag chair! Who would like to sit in it today? Oh, my goodness! All of you? Great. All you have to do is choose to be quiet during circle time. I will see who can make that good choice. Come to the rug, children."*

Bribe from Mrs. Oakes:

> Roger: *"Mom! Mrs. Oakes said I could be excused early on Friday for the basketball tournament if I finish that biology project I didn't do last week. I thought she wasn't going to let me go!"*

Self-managing for a reward:

> Roger: *"Mom! Mrs. Oakes spoke with me about getting out early on Friday for the basketball tournament. I thought she wasn't going to let me go, but she gave me a choice. She said that I could choose to finish the biology project due last week by Wednesday. She's going to grade it right away. If it's not at least B-level work, I'll have to improve it by Friday. I'm going to do it. I already told Coach Daniels that I'll be there."*

Bribes minimize accomplishment:

Mr. Fox decided to give an MP3 player as a prize to the student who he judged wrote the best essay about how Martin Luther King Jr.'s life still mattered today. Brody won the prize. He was surprised beyond words and very happy. Brody felt sure that he was the only one among his fifth-grade classmates who did not have an MP3 player.

Brody's classmates crowded around him to see it.

Brody's mom and dad said: *"Congratulations! Good work! See? You can do it!"*

Brody's aunt said: *"Wow, Brody! I will send you five dollars for your good work."*

Mr. Fox said: *"Brody, your writing showed great and surprising improvement."*

No one asked Brody where he got his ideas or what books he used for the information about Dr. King. No one asked if he rewrote it many times. There was no mention of his vocabulary choice. Brody did not think about or ever say what *he* liked best about his finished work. Brody's *accomplishment* took a distant second place to the prize. An easy opportunity to use a wonderful reward to increase Brody's self-esteem and reinforce his self-management skills was missed.

Bribes decrease motivation:

Mrs. Snow, to Mrs. Quinn, Jamal's first-grade teacher: *"How did you ever get Jamal through the day last year? I'm just about done trying. He makes learning difficult for everyone and sets a bad example, too. My reward system doesn't work with him at all."*

Mrs. Quinn: *"He was a handful last year, too. What system do you use?"*

Mrs. Snow: *"Each morning, everyone gets a plastic jar with five pretend jelly beans inside. Every time they misbehave, they have to turn in one jelly bean, meaning they really get five chances to have their behavior mistakes overlooked. I think that's plenty of leeway. At the end of the day they get to trade however many jelly beans they have left for real ones. But, Jamal uses all of his chances before mid-morning snack. After that, his behavior is worse and worse, and then others who have lost their jelly beans join him."*

Mrs. Quinn: *"Yes, I discovered that without some kind of incentive, I could not make him behave, either. Anyway, there was never any lasting behavior change once he got the reward. The same was true for other kids. As you say, once they use up all of their 'chances,' they have nothing to lose.*

"I decided to try taking away all 'rewards for good behavior' from everybody. Instead, I started this with my whole class: Every morning I gave them four color-coded cards—one for each learning activity in my room. Each card had two choices on it to use at the activity center when it was time to be there. I tried to make each choice appealing for different interests. No choice depended on behavior. When anyone misbehaved during an activity, I began asking them to tell me if they made a bad choice. 'Choices' became the watchword for all of my dealings with misbehavior. It took a while for this to catch on, but even Jamal was better because I took the rewards for good behavior away. He was equal to everyone else all day. Sometimes I still had to bring him to my desk to 'talk' or 'do me a favor' to separate him from the group. But I can tell you this—the choice system works better for me than the reward system. When I do give rewards, the children seem able to appreciate them more."

All students have opportunities to feel rewarded or punished because of personal behavior many times during a typical school day. It may seem, at first, that the end result is the same whether the feeling is the product of a bribe or of free choice. But the difference is significant and essentially different.

Bribes are controllers that keep power in the hands of the teacher offering the bribe. *The teacher* judges the action worthy or not. Students, then, have the option of blaming the teacher for an end result that is unwanted. They can and do attribute favoritism, meanness, unfairness, and misunderstanding as replacements for personal responsibility.

Helping students recognize that it is their right and privilege to make responsible choices changes their perception of both good and bad outcomes. The capricious nature of "earning" or "not earning" a reward is erased, as is the option to blame someone else. Teaching students about self-determination through the exercise of free choice is a gift that lasts a lifetime.

Fairness is Based on Need, Merit, and Equality

The expression "That's not fair!" is familiar to anyone who works in a school setting.

Students say it to teachers, teachers say it to administrators, administrators say it to the central office. The intent is the same. Something perceived as unjust, biased, or inequitable needs remedy. By implication, the remedy will bring resolution and relief that satisfies the Golden Rule: "Do unto others as you would have them do unto you." It is the concept of fairness that students know best when they come to school for the first time.

Students rightfully expect there to be no "teacher's pet." They expect equality and tolerance. Everyone will and should be treated exactly the same according to their untrained concept of fairness. They are quick to allow themselves opportunity to be the exception to that rule but slow to afford that opportunity to anyone else.

To use rewards that influence behavior effectively, applying the wider meaning of fairness is necessary. *The first step is teaching by word and example that it is fair to meet someone's need and it is fair to reward someone's outstanding effort or accomplishment.* From the beginning of the school year, teachers should intentionally, consistently, obviously, and frequently demonstrate that a classroom community is about much more than equal treatment.

At first, the teacher's word and example will show that each class member's uniqueness will be celebrated. Then, things such as giving a birthday memento, holding up a drawing, repeating a joke or riddle a student told (saying his or her name aloud), mentioning several favorites of different students, showing joy at an individual's answer to a question, or teaching about someone's religious holiday can set the stage for students' realization that they and their teacher should enjoy one another.

All students need to *experience* how need and merit are legitimate applications of fairness. Whenever possible, students should be participants in delivering a needed service or rewarding a deserving classmate. Doing so builds classroom community unlike anything else. Teachers' direct, unapologetic, and warm response to concerned students eases their natural jealousy and desire to receive a gift or service awarded to someone else.

Notice that if teachers or students meet someone's need or reward an outstanding effort or accomplishment, it is not a bribe! It is a *fair* use of an opportunity to be selfless and considerate of someone else. Teachers report that using rewards in this way affords them freedom to be kinder, more generous and creative in forming a learning environment that is more trusting and less controlling and manipulative.

Trust grows as teachers' consistent actions demonstrate that they *know and care* about every student inside and outside of class:

Outside of class example:

Mrs. Jenner, school social worker, to Mrs. Russell, seventh-grade teacher: *"Sherman is coming back from his long-term suspension on Monday. Maybe this information will help you help him. Turned out that the day he got into that fight when someone took his milk at breakfast had to do with the fact that he was truly hungry. There was a fire in the house where he lived with his grandfather. They were still living in it even though there was a huge hole in the roof, and it was freezing cold. There was no food in the house at all. Child Services had picked up Sherman's little brother outside the house wandering bare-footed the day before. Right now, he's living with his aunt. The younger children are in foster care. Mom is not in the picture at all. He did not get into any other trouble while he was at the Tutoring Center."*

Mrs. Russell: *"My goodness, I don't know what to say. Sherman is an excellent math student, but he's failing my English class. He's missing so many assignments. If I can get him to talk, he's pretty vocal, but mostly, he's just shut down."*

Mrs. Jenner: *"School seems to be at least one place for him to find some support and success. I hope we can help him in that way. I know you'll do what you can."*

Mrs. Russell put three new pocket folders with a new schedule, pen, a few pencils, some paper, and a giant-sized Kit Kat bar inside on Sherman's desk for Monday. She also wrote this note:

Welcome back, Sherman! I missed you. You probably think there's no way you can pass English now, but I think you can do it. I have some ideas about what you can do. Will you please see me today so we can plan a time to meet? Am I remembering right that you like Kit Kats? I hope you have a good day.

Sherman did not stop by on his own, but Mrs. Russell looked for him during lunch and asked him again to come to see her. He did. At the meeting, Mrs. Russell asked Sherman what he thought he needed to do to pass English. He did not know. Mrs. Russell asked him if he was willing to do what she had written on a short list of amended assignments that would make him feel successful for the next month and give him hope for the remaining months of school.

To her credit, Mrs. Russell knew Sherman's need and set aside the mountain of required English curriculum Sherman failed to do. She exercised uncommon common sense by designing "fair" academic work for him that preserved his self-esteem while he worked toward a reachable goal. They agreed to meet again after the first assignment was due.

In-class example:

> Charley, to his second-grade teacher: *"How come we have to copy all this stuff in our notebook and Jodi doesn't?"*
>
> Mr. Rose: *"Charley, I think you know. Why does Jodi read from large-print books? Why does Julie help Jodi on the playground? Why does she sit in the front row?"*
>
> Charley: *"Because she has trouble and can't see good."*
>
> Mr. Rose: *"That's right. She can't see well. So why does she get to have a special notebook?"*
>
> Charley: *"Because of her eyes. But you put her name and some stickers on her notebook cover."*
>
> Mr. Rose: *"I did, Charley. I just felt like being nice. Have I ever been nice to you?"*
>
> Charley: *"Yes. You gave me that yellow pencil with the smiley faces."*
>
> Mr. Rose: *"You answered your own question, buddy. Now, keep up your good work."*

Teachers discover that introducing fairness based on need and merit in addition to equality opens new doors for using rewards that offer support and relationship. Students experience and observe their teachers' kind attention to individual needs. Jealousy, pouting, and whining about "unfairness" lessens. Instead, a classroom community begins to grow.

WAYS TO USE REWARDS TO REINFORCE RELATIONSHIPS

Any consideration about rewards as motivators to learn or to be instruments of behavior change gives rise to an important reminder: behavior and motivation are proprietary and singular. *Who can change behavior? Only the person who owns it.* True motivation is an *intrinsic force.* It is a feeling of enthusiasm, interest, or commitment that causes a person to direct and activate his energies toward a desired end.

The adage "You can lead a horse to water, but you can't make him drink" surfaces when teachers' frustration peaks. It is a comforting analogy—comforting, because it represents resignation, surrender, and even release from responsibility to influence resistant students who lack motivation to behave and/or learn. However, lurking behind the truth of that saying is another maxim for teachers: "If you make students thirsty, when you lead them to water they will drink it."

An unlimited number of intrinsic factors activate students' willingness to comply with rules, cooperate, engage in learning, act responsibly, help others, lead their peers, and modify their own behavior. Some factors are specific to an individual; others are common motivators welcomed universally. For example, feeling appreciated, competent, successful, and loved creates an unrivaled sense of well-being and self-worth.

Rewards have a place in schools! Bribes do not. Use rewards *spontaneously* every day.

Rewards from teachers should be pleasant surprises. Give them to the entire class as well as individuals. *Be sure they do not represent payment for a required or expected behavior. Use them to connect with students by unexpected actions that demonstrate acknowledgment of their need to feel appreciated, competent, successful, and loved.*

The following five examples show how rewards that connect to intrinsic motivators might look:

1. Mrs. Clark gave all of her first-grade students a teddy bear eraser after recess. She told them it was because she thought of them in the store. She did not connect the prizes to their cooperation on the playground or to their good behavior.
2. Mr. O'Dell began putting several stickers on everybody's math homework paper, whether the work was 100 percent or not. The stickers were just a joyful gesture. He found he could mix in messages to individual students, too—*"You can do it!" "Needs improvement!" "Keep up the good work."* Every paper had a positive message.
3. Ms. Duffy began writing brief notes every day on cheery paper to her students for just about any reason. They did not take much time, and the good will they fostered was worth the effort. Here are some of them:

> *Dear Leticia,*
> *Congratulations on the 100 percent you earned on the English grammar test. Mr. Verne said you were also a terrific coach for your classmates before the test. I'm happy you could help in that way. I like knowing you and watching you in class.*

> *Dear Bernedette,*
> *What a nice surprise to hear from you! I was not surprised you thanked me for the candy bar. I could tell during our meeting that your mom taught you many things at home that make you the nice girl you are. I'll tell her that in person if I get to meet her at Open House. I put*

*the little drawing you made on my desk. When I see it, it will remind
me of you!*

Dear Pernell,
*This note will tell you what I don't seem to find time to tell you after
class. It's this: I am happy to be your teacher. I admire the way you do
your work, and I do notice how patient you are when others need more
time to finish their work. You are growing up to be a young man who is
not only intelligent but kind. Congratulations, Pernell. You have every
reason to be proud.*

4. Since September, Karen displayed hostile behavior in Mrs. Rodriguez's class. She was argumentative and disrespectful whenever asked to come to attention or participate. She was frequently sent out of class. Mrs. Rodriguez met with Karen and put this note in a green folder (Karen's favorite color) following their meeting:

   Dear Karen,
   *Until we had a chance to talk, I could not know how many hard things
   you have to deal with in your everyday life. I want you to know I
   admire you for all you do and understand better why you are so quick
   to be angry. I hope you feel better knowing that you could learn a
   number of ways to control your temper. Thank you for agreeing to let
   Ms. Mulligan work on that with you. I'll go with you to meet her, don't
   worry. I will try to be more patient and know you will try harder to
   control yourself, also. Thank you for coming to see me.*

5. Just before the Thanksgiving holiday break, Mr. Frank offered a surprise to his class. Instead of science class, he formed a circle with his class and said something positive about each student as a thank-you to them for being in his class. He then asked others to do the same if they wished to offer a thank-you to someone else. Afterward, they enjoyed a piece of cake frosted with this message: Happy Thanksgiving—Remember to Count Your Blessings.

Some might say instructional time is too limited to allow a departure from it that would take so much time. Others would argue that the affective development of students is as important as cognitive development. Teachers who choose to depart from required curriculum on occasion feel that students' response and the positive after-effects are well worth the sacrifice.

This chapter offers this reward: Enjoy the magical results from using rewards that have no contingencies attached. To use rewards in this way is to practice the art of teaching at its highest level. Students begin to view their teachers as trustworthy adults from whom they can draw strength. Spontaneous rewards enable teachers to relate to and raise students' conscious awareness of their power to choose and self-regulate. Some of the most cherished prizes of the teaching profession are satisfaction, joy, and being a life-changing influence. It is interesting to note that students control these prizes.

POINTS TO REMEMBER

- Allowing and excusing reliance on extrinsic motivators for a short-term fix to control behavior creates a burden of long-term misbehavior cycles that require an endless use of coercion, threats, demands, and greater rewards.
- Rewards that cause one to act or not act *to get the reward* are bribes. They diminish or replace free choice—the bedrock of intrinsic motivation.
- Students can and should learn that equal treatment is fair, as is meeting someone's need and rewarding someone's outstanding effort or accomplishment.
- Teachers who *only use rewards spontaneously* have discovered how easily and effectively they make students feel appreciated, competent, successful, and loved.

NOTES

1. Kohn, Alfie. *Punished by Rewards.* New York: Houghton Mifflin Company, 1993.
2. Deci, Edward L., and Richard Flaste. *Why We Do What We Do.* New York: Penguin Books, 1996.

Chapter 7

Knowing Me, Knowing You—It's the Right Thing to Do

If there are obstacles, the shortest line between two points may be the crooked one.
—*Bertolt Brecht, German dramatist (1886–1956)*

Every teacher who confronts resistant learners recognizes the challenge posed in attempting to solve the dilemma of *why* students refuse to engage in the necessary learning process. Curricular requirements do not change, so each passing day leaves the students in question farther and farther behind. This increases the frustration and understandable desire of teachers to find a "quick fix" for a complex problem. There is none.

Reaching resistant learners so that teaching the required curricula can happen occurs when teachers find a way to break down the barrier of resistance. Every opportunity has potential. It takes time, patience, trial and error, and several attempts to find a way. It involves knowing as much as possible about the student for whom instruction is not working.

A *positive personal connection* between teacher and student allows the teacher a sphere of influence strong enough that the student will discover a reason to try to change his behavior. That self-selected attempt to change is the victory! It should not be considered a lesser victory than completing the required curricula successfully—the sacred grail of school systems.

In the quest to find a way to break down the barriers surrounding resistant learners, research in the field of learning styles and multiple intelligences can be most helpful. It recognizes and describes individual differences in learning preferences and areas of strength. Any teacher can use this information to focus on a resistant student's learning profile. In that concentrated look, the teacher may discover something upon which to begin a *positive personal connection.*

Learning styles and multiple intelligences offer a large variety of tools for teachers' use, describing how individual differences in cognitive ability and skills can and should be measured and accompanied by assessment instruments for identifying learning preferences. Cautionary studies warn that not nearly enough hard evidence exists to support claims of increased learning even when teaching matches students' preferred learning styles.[1]

Nonetheless, years of work in the field support concepts of learning styles and multiple intelligences with studies that show their significant impact on student learning. A variety of programs offer teachers specific ways to appreciate, accept, and accommodate student differences. They identify and legitimize the real-life experience of learners young and old who have wondered why learning with one teacher was so much easier than learning with another.

MULTIPLE INTELLIGENCES: GIFTS, TALENTS, SPECIAL INTERESTS, AND WAYS OF THINKING

Howard Gardner's lifetime of research has challenged the belief that individuals are born with a certain potential intelligence that is unchangeable but measurable by intelligence test results that reveal present and future cognitive capacity. Instead, Gardner's investigation into human intelligence led him to develop specific criteria for defining a *set* of human intelligences. To date, he has defined eight abilities or intelligences: *linguistic, logical-mathematical, musical, spatial, bodily-kinesthetic, interpersonal, intrapersonal, and naturalist.*[2]

Gardner's theory of multiple intelligences emphasizes that individuals have all of the eight intelligences to greater or lesser degrees. Each intelligence represents an existing or emerging strength. Sometimes, a gift, talent, special interest, or preferred way of thinking stands out in a person at an early age. Expressions such as "She is a gifted musician" or "He is unusually talented in art" or "I don't think anyone knows more about baseball" are common.

Personality, temperament, and life experiences are just some of the factors that define and refine each individual's intelligence profile. The ideas behind multiple intelligences have created multiple tools for teachers. There are lesson plans, charts, graphs, student assessments, school and district-wide programs designed to enhance pedagogy and increase student learning.[3]

If a teacher is searching for a way to reach a resistant learner, then noticing whatever gifts, talents, or special interests that student may have is an easy way to make a positive personal connection. Using existing or emerging strengths to engage the student in frequent conversation comes next. Attention, approval, and genuine interest offered by the teacher is much more influential than insincere or distracted praise.

If a positive personal connection occurs, the student's resistance lessens because the student perceives the teacher as caring and supportive. The chance for the student to choose to self-modify his behavior increases.

Each year, a classroom of students allows every teacher the opportunity to experience firsthand how multiple intelligences reveal themselves. Some students are nearly uncontrollably social; others are clearly artistic, athletic, musical, or remarkable math students. Multiple intelligences provide a welcome explanation for the wide range of individual differences among students in every class.

In this example, Jeremy displays strength in spatial intelligence:

Mrs. Benson (elementary principal): *"Hello, Jeremy! You are here so early today. How come?"*

Jeremy: *"Same thing."*

Mrs. Benson: *"Hmmm . . . same thing as yesterday? Were you drawing during learning time, again?"*

Jeremy: *"Yup."*

Mrs. Benson: *"What were you drawing this time?"*

Jeremy: *"A car. She tore it up and threw it away."*

Mrs. Benson: *"I know you can draw cars very well. Look—I still have the one you drew for me taped to my cabinet. It's really good. Are you going to draw new cars for a big car company when you grow up?"*

Jeremy: *"Dunno. Maybe."*

Mrs. Benson: *"Tell me again why drawing cars instead of paying attention makes Mrs. Hawkins so unhappy."*

Jeremy: *"Because I don't hear what I'm supposed to do when she's all done talking."*

Mrs. Benson: *"Yes, and even more important, you don't know what she's talking about, so you aren't learning."*

Jeremy: *"She talks too long. It's boring."*

The resolution of the incident in this example is not as important as noting that Mrs. Benson, the principal, is the one making the positive personal connection with Jeremy. Jeremy gets to feel that Mrs. Benson appreciates whatever his art ability is and because of that, she gets to address the matter at hand—his disconnection from learning.

By tearing up his drawing, Mrs. Hawkins, in her frustration, has lost the chance to use Jeremy's penchant for drawing as a possible relationship builder that could motivate Jeremy to cooperate more than he does. If drawing is Jeremy's only noticeable strength at this time, the loss of that connection would be significant.

LEARNING STYLES: PREFERENCES AFFECT LEARNING BEHAVIORS

Carl Jung's research on psychological types, first published in 1921, asserted that four behavioral functions describe how people receive information and then judge what personal significance it may hold for them.

1. *Sensory Thinkers* perceive information primarily through their senses and depend on their *intellect* to assess its personal usefulness. They are most comfortable with facts, analysis, practicality, and the purposeful application of ideas.
2. *Sensory Feelers* perceive information primarily through their senses and depend on their *feelings* to assess its personal usefulness. They also are most comfortable with facts, but they become meaningful through reliance on personal warmth, social interaction, helping others, and collaborating with them.
3. *Intuitive Thinkers* perceive information *instinctively*; actual evidence is secondary to what they know or believe. They prefer to assess the personal usefulness of ideas, people, and circumstances in terms of possibilities. They are most comfortable with analysis, logic, ingenuity, and critical, independent thought.
4. *Intuitive Feelers* also perceive information instinctively, and possibilities energize them. However, they judge the personal usefulness of information primarily through *feelings*. Personal warmth, imagination, flexibility, and insightful interaction with others characterize this psychological type.

Jung also asserted that a person's perception and judgment are modified further depending on whether they live more comfortably in most situations as introverts or extroverts.[4]

Well-known in the learning styles arena, authors Robert Hanson and Harvey Silver researched and developed a comprehensive model for teachers. The Thoughtful Education Model is designed to recognize "both the cognitive and affective demands of learning," and is based on the four paired Jungian functions. Detailed exercises, diagnostic instruments, and self-analysis questions identify and specify characteristics of teaching styles and learning styles.[5]

This program and others like it provide yet another tool teachers can use first as a self-study. In addition, the model shows how to develop one student's or all students' learning profile based on a preferred learning mode. Most students (and many teachers) are unaware of their dependency on certain ways of thinking and learning; they know their preferences only by intuition.

It is important to note that the differences between and among different styles of learning are significant. One style is not more legitimate than another. However, it is always perceived to be that way by the person whose preferred style is the opposite of someone else's.

> As an adult, Jean vividly recalls the teacher who singled her out every Friday for having the messiest desk in her class. In truth, papers, books, folders, notebooks continually fought for position and carried their battle onto the floor around her desk. When needed, a pen or pencil was never at hand.
>
> She remembers wanting to be Rosemarie, who sat across from her and personified neatness and organization in every way. Her sharpened pencils, erasers intact, were in a green case—no smudges ever appeared on her papers! Jean's teacher honored Rosemarie's request to move away from her because Rosemarie found her to be such a source of annoyance and distraction. Throughout her school years, Jean does not remember anyone who helped her unlock the mystery of how to become organized.

Teachers naturally tend to set up their classrooms to their liking. Consciously or not, their preferred style of learning will be evident in its final appearance.

> In September, charts, graphs, posters, borders, bulletin boards, windows, desks, and even ceiling pictures left no question about Mrs. Baker's creativity. It was artfully busy. Upon seeing it, Mr. Green, the school counselor, gently reminded her again that students with ADHD such as Doreen and Sherod might find the environment a bit overstimulating. Mrs. Baker said, "I really like my classroom this way. I think my students look forward to being in my class because it is so interesting. Do you have suggestions for what I can do to help Sherod and Doreen without undoing all that I've done here?"

The instructional style most comfortable to teachers is that of their own learning style. The strategies and assessment procedures they use are likely to reflect the same.

Mrs. Mason was rightfully worried that her new team teacher, Mr. Jerzak, might be a poor match. One look in his room told her that having tables and chairs, work spaces, and so many materials in open view would be distracting to their mutual students. There was so much factual material to cover in the curriculum! Once he saw the rows of desks in her room, perhaps he would see how easily that setup allows attention to be monitored. Students need to be responsible for their own work. Daily tests and quizzes are the excellent indicators of learning. Group learning? There is nothing about it that's truly reliable.

Every learning and teaching style has merit and will be received by others with greater or lesser enthusiasm depending on their personal preference. The teaching styles of both teachers, while challenging to them as partners, present a fortunate opportunity for students. The best learners and teachers are those exposed to a variety of learning environments, teaching strategies, evaluation methods, and personalities.

Teachers who know the implications of each learning style are in a marvelous position of power:

- They can differentiate instruction more easily.

    Mr. Amina recognizes that Joe, Mitzi, Shanda, and Edguardo are the "talkers" in his class and love to pair-share, collaborate, and help others, often to the point of distraction. With that in mind, at the start of today's class he will allow some time to everyone who wishes to meet and make suggestions to improve the final draft of their book report.

- They can anticipate problems that some students will have in a given lesson or assignment.

    An excellent student, Delmar usually "loses" math homework assignments designed for drill and practice. The day's geometry lesson has homework for drill and practice. For homework, Mrs. Saxby asks Delmar to write an essay on the origins of Euclidean geometry, leaving its length or brevity up to Delmar. She knows his interest and competence in analysis, writing, and research. She correctly guessed that he spent more time on the essay than he ever would have on the drill and practice assignment.

- They can engage all but the youngest students in meaningful conversation by explaining the significance of their preferences as they relate to learning and study habits.

    Mrs. Allan to Jerome: "Jerome, when you asked, 'What if the British didn't win the war?' in class today, it made me smile. Almost everyone else rolled their eyes. I like how your mind always takes you to considering a different side of things. I don't know if you have ever heard of divergent thinking. It means that you like to think creatively by exploring other possibilities. It's a wonderful mind-set to have, and the world needs thinkers like you who like to find unexpected solutions to problems. Do you think you are creative?"

If teachers recognize the self-talk that prompts their first emotional reactions to challenging situations, they are more likely to reframe a response that favors a rational solution. Doing so helps forge relationships with students whose self-talk is different, or even opposite, from their own. In that same way, teachers who are aware of the strengths and weaknesses of their own learning preferences and teaching style have many options from which to draw when trying to reach a resistant learner.

RESISTANT LEARNERS OR RESISTANT TEACHERS?

Students whose preferred mode of learning is *opposite* that of their teacher will find themselves struggling to compensate for their teacher's preferred teaching mode. It can and does happen that an entire school year can pass where a teacher's dominant teaching style fails completely to include any teaching strategies, lesson plans, activities, assignments, projects, or assessments that provide opportunities to learn in different styles.

For whatever reasons, when teachers make no attempt to recognize or accommodate the true needs of the students in their charge, school feels like a forced march toward failure. It does not take long for students to resist the learning process altogether. Attributing personal dislike to the teacher further strengthens the barrier that protects resisters from feeling incompetent and inadequate. The stage is set for conflict.

Sometimes, it is that disconnection, and *only* that disconnection, that causes a student to give up on the learning process. It answers parents' oft-repeated question, "What is happening? She had such a good year last year."

In the examples that follow, something that each student needs is missing, and an opportunity for the teacher to make a positive personal connection is present.

Example #1

Mrs. Hanigan, Tim's mom, to Tim's dad: "*Joe, Mrs. Daly called and said Tim is twenty-seven pages behind in his reading workbook! How could that happen? She said it's full of toy car drawings. She's going to send it home, and we're supposed to help him catch up.*"

Before calling Tim's mom, Mrs. Daly should take a minute to think about him. Is he a capable student? Is he bored? What interests him most during the school day? Is he disorganized and likely to be forgetting his workbook? How *did* he get so far behind? Decide whether every workbook page needs completion.

This is the opportunity: Speak with Tim first and do something unexpected to offset his anticipation of trouble. Engage him in pleasant, non-threatening conversation as much as possible. Offer undivided attention.

> Mrs. Daly: *"Tim, do you have a collection of toy cars? I thought so! You know how to draw them so well. How many cars do you think you have? Wow! What is your favorite one like? I've been looking at your workbook. I guess you've been drawing more than you've been working! How come? I'm sorry I didn't notice, and now lots of your workbook pages are empty. What should we do about this? How can I help you? I'm going to write down what we're going to do."*

Follow-up is essential. Keep the car connection active. Be careful not to set up a bribe as part of the plan—*"After you finish x number of pages, I'll give you a toy car or a picture of one or some other prize."* Do consider giving Tim a prize for progress, but make it be a spontaneous act of generosity on your part that he deserves because he is Tim trying to improve, not because he wants a promised reward.

Example #2

> Mr. Alexander, Reuben's dad: *"Explain yourself, Reuben. You know that a D in math is not acceptable. What's going on?"*

> Reuben: *"Dad, I just don't get it. I got stuck with Mr. Fox. He explains the proofs over and over, but I don't understand how he gets the answer. I've stayed for extra help, but he just says the same thing, only louder. I just can't do it and I don't care anymore."*

Mr. Alexander may or may not call Mr. Fox to express his concern. Either way, Mr. Fox has two opportunities. The first is to look inward and open his mind to the possibility that his teaching style is too limited. This self-examination lurks in every teacher's heart when several students fail to learn the curriculum as it is presented. So many teacher tools are available to help teachers capture and activate the learning potential of students. Mr. Fox should be intentional about learning from them.

Mr. Fox's second opportunity is to meet with Reuben to help him identify what he thinks may be preventing him for earning a successful grade. Reuben claims he "does not care anymore." Generally, when students use that well-worn phrase, they really mean they have lost hope. Reuben does care. His father cares.

Mr. Fox could certainly challenge Reuben's expectation of teachers who can't teach him successfully by beginning the meeting with an apology.

Mr. Fox: *"Reuben, thank you for meeting with me. I want to begin by saying I am really sorry that my teaching does not seem to be matching your way of learning very well. No, don't shake your head. I really mean it. I know that you have been a successful math student. I am hoping you will improve your grade during the next semester. I want to help you be successful. Here is one idea.*

"With your permission, I'd like to ask Rakeem to help you before or after school for a while. He always wants to explain the proofs to me in several different ways. I think that he might explain things differently from me to your benefit. What do you think of my idea?"

Any practical suggestion that offers Reuben a ray of hope would indicate Mr. Fox's sincere desire to help. It would only take his continued interest and support to motivate Reuben to begin trying again. That, coupled with some easy conversation about sports or music (or any other teen topic), would likely change Reuben's negative perception of Mr. Fox as a teacher and person. It would be a positive personal connection.

It is true that some students' cognitive development is not mature enough for some abstract concepts. However, all of Mr. Fox's students have a ticket for the train. It is his professional responsibility to see that all of his students get on board.

Example #3

Mr. Knight, to Shandra's parents: *"In my opinion, Shandra only wants to talk. She's not interested in learning at all. I have changed her seat four times this month. If she's quiet, she's looking out the window. She will fail English if she doesn't straighten up. She needs to be a bit more respectful when I correct her."*

Mr. and Mrs. Daniels: *"She has never failed English before. She loves poetry and drama. She has a leading role in the school play this year. We know she's a social girl, but no teacher has ever said she's disrespectful. We'll speak to her about that and it will stop. What else can we do?"*

Mr. Knight: *"Tell her to pay attention and be quiet."*

Mr. Knight is a no-nonsense teacher, well known for his full command of the English curriculum. His lesson plans are purposeful and organized. His expectation is that students will follow his directives, memorize the rules for grammar and usage, and learn to follow his format *only* for writing essays or book reports. He is not particularly interested in knowing his students personally, and fervently wishes they would leave their issues at the door when they come to class.

Mr. Knight's strengths are Shandra's weaknesses. Opportunities for expressing personal feelings, using imagination, exploring possibilities, and social interaction would be obvious motivators for Shandra. When motivating opportunities are missing, students such as Shandra mistakenly take their absence to mean that their teacher does not like them. Learning suffers.

Connecting with Shandra would mean that Mr. Knight decides that the time, effort, and energy it would take for him to step out of his tried-and-true teaching persona would be worth it. In this case, forming a positive personal connection with Shandra may not be possible or crucial.

Realistically, Shandra will likely survive the school year in Mr. Knight's class with lower than average grades. Luckily, she has her parents' support and so does Mr. Knight. Mr. Knight will likely view Shandra and others like her as the necessary distractions to his teaching style that they are to him.

Example #4

Mrs. Starski was excited to spend four weeks teaching the Civil War unit in a new way. She carefully designed behavioral objectives, activities, and assessments that were tailor-made to suit the gifts, talents, special interests, ways of thinking, and learning preferences for each student in her class. For example, students could research Abraham Lincoln's role in the war. Some students could memorize and deliver the Gettysburg Address in costume. Others could create a poster that featured the Emancipation Proclamation. A student group could present the causes of the war from the viewpoint of the South, the North, farmers, southern belles, and slaves. Still others could create a *Jeopardy* game to aid factual recall.

Rosa to Juan (seventh grade): *"What did you get on the Civil War test?*

Juan: *"C."*

Rosa: *"Ooooh, Juan! You never get Cs. You will be in trouble with your mom if she finds out."*

Juan: *"I know. Mrs. Starski didn't even teach about the causes of the Civil War. Did she give us notes to study? No! When I asked her about it, she said I should have paid better attention when Serena, Nate, and Alice gave their presentations about three causes of the war. Who knew? Do you even remember their presentations? That's not teaching. I hate her class. I told her so, too. She needed to give us notes, like other teachers. That's the best way to study: notes from the teacher."*

Juan was unable to extrapolate the "need-to-know" information from the array of presentations that evolved from everyone's participation in the Civil War unit. Juan's emotional response to his unusual low grade and his out-of-character bold accusations invited two responses from Mrs. Starski when Juan approached her desk after class.

Her first *thought* came immediately from her long-established inner speech about "children knowing their place." *"How does he dare speak to me that way?"* was followed by *feeling* angry, and perhaps hurt and unappreciated. *"After all the work I did to create an outstanding unit . . ."* could well have led to an *action*, *"Don't question my teaching ability, young man! You have said enough. You can expect a phone call home about your disrespect."*

Instead, Mrs. Starski chose to reframe her exchange with Juan, hoping to turn what felt like a negative encounter into a positive one. Her second thought, *"It's unusual for Juan to act out this way. I will try to use this as a teachable moment because this kind of outburst can grow into resentment that lasts too long,"* was followed by feeling open to his criticism: *"He really does depend on structure—guess there wasn't enough guided instruction for him. . ."* leading to this action:

> Mrs. Starski: *"Juan, just have a seat here for a minute. I'm having trouble hearing what you are saying because you are so upset. This is what I think you want me to know. Please listen and tell me if I'm right. You are upset by your low test grade. You think I should have done a better job of teaching the facts you needed to know. You wish I had given you a study guide. Am I right?"*

Conversation ensues. Juan is calmer. Mrs. Starski chooses a resolution. Before the encounter ends, Mrs. Starski addresses the way Juan presented his concern and helps him state his concerns more appropriately. She may even choose to share what her first thought/feeling/action plan was. Both Juan and Mrs. Starski know each other better in the end.

All teachers and students can and should learn to adapt to other learning styles. It happens predominantly by default. However, teachers who are adept at presenting lessons that are effective for every learning style have an advantage. They can be intentional in promoting the higher levels of achievement possible when learners can integrate the best facets of different styles into their learning experience. By so doing, a well-balanced, educated student emerges—someone who can live peaceably in the desirable middle between crippling reliance on one's own learning preference and intolerance of others' learning behaviors.

To know one another and to be known is a hallmark of being human. At every turn, teachers should explore whatever avenue provides an opportunity to make a positive personal connection with resistant learners. Viewing resistant learners in the light of their gifts, talents, special interests, ways of thinking, and preferred modes of learning takes much less time, effort, and energy than dealing with their refusal to learn or cooperate, respond to, or comply with daily instruction. Teachers who step out of their comfort zone to open learners' closed doors receive a lifetime achievement award every time it happens.

POINTS TO REMEMBER

- Positive personal connections, especially between teachers and resistant students, will help break the barriers that prevent them from choosing not to learn.
- Attention, approval, and genuine interest offered by teachers to students for their gifts, talents, and/or special interest is a sure way to make a positive personal connection.
- The differences between and among different styles of learning are significant; *every* learning and teaching style has merit and will be received by others with greater or lesser enthusiasm depending on their personal preference.
- Teachers do bear the responsibility for becoming knowledgeable and skillful enough to present lessons that honor *all* styles of learning.

NOTES

1. Woolfolk, Anita. *Educational Psychology.* Upper Saddle River, NJ: Pearson Education, Ltd., 2010.
2. Gardner, Howard. *Frames of Mind.* New York: Basic Books, 2011.
3. Silver, Harvey F., Richard W. Strong, and Matthew J. Perini. *So Each May Learn.* Alexandria, VA: Association for Supervision and Curriculum Development, 2000.
4. Jung, Carl G. *Psychological Types.* Princeton, NJ: Princeton University Press, 1921.
5. Silver, Harvey F., and Richard W. Strong. *Learning Styles and Strategies.* Trenton, NJ: Thoughtful Education Press, 1996.

Chapter 8

Three Rs—Don't Leave Home Without Them

A limit on what you will do, puts a limit on what you can do.
—*Anonymous*

Professional teachers answer the question "Why did I become a teacher?" many times throughout their career. Sometimes it arises when the weight of bureaucracy threatens to crush all hope. Regulations that force teachers to "teach to the test" squeeze the creativity from lesson planning; students' stressed and weary faces reflect their teachers' discouragement. At other times, the question begs an existential answer from teachers who reexamine the root causes for their career choice.

Love of learning, teaching important content material, treasured family tradition, affecting global change through education, and daily proximity to children's joy and innocence are among many worthy reasons offered. Whatever the reasons, all teachers face the same demands, so many in number, as to make even the most stout-hearted observer recognize that becoming a teacher is not a choice for the faint of heart.

When asked, "Why do you teach?," most teachers' answers include telling about interactions with a student or a class. These memorable events, situations, or accomplishments best explain why teachers make a commitment to such an exacting profession. Each account that follows confirms the pleasure and power of teaching:

Ms. Lucity: *"Without a doubt, it's being with the children. Today, eyes dancing and jumping up and down, Lucia told me it was going to be the best day of her life so far because I picked her name out of Dr. Seuss's hat to have lunch with me."*

Mr. Howard: *"I am energized by young people. English literature and poetry lend themselves to discussion, self-discovery, laughter, and tears. I watch my students learn to talk and listen, form convictions and defend their viewpoints. I feel I am making a difference."*

Mrs. Widay: *"Some moments make vivid memories that will last my life-time. For two years, in seventh and eighth grades, I begged, cajoled, and threatened Sheila to make her speak loudly enough to be heard. It was painful for us all to wait and be patient and repeat what she said. At the end of eighth grade, Sheila, wearing a paper stovepipe hat, perfectly recited Lincoln's Gettysburg Address from memory, in a booming voice. There was total silence. Then applause. It brought tears to more eyes than mine."*

Long after Sheila's accomplishment, Mrs. Widay learned that during those two years, Sheila had been working through her grief at the unexpected death of her father. No one at school knew.

The curricula for each grade level requires teachers to create lessons that specify proper objectives accompanied by procedures and materials that enhance everyone's learning, and that can be proved effective by immediate and long-term evaluations. A *controlled* environment that is calm and safe is the expected primary goal of classroom management plans. This part of "schooling," as important as it is, often occupies center stage exclusively, leaving the lead players—*students deserving consideration as unique individuals and teachers who want to make positive personal connections with them*—in the wings.

Resistant learners, especially, are the lucky ones if they have one of the bravest and best teachers who reclaim center stage by their firm resolve to create a community in their classroom where "students first" is the goal. Management evolves from cooperation and participation; discipline is rooted in responsibility for free choices.

Students are well aware that they are not all the same. They will ultimately accept or reject personal differences or differing needs of others based on how their teacher does. A hint of impatience, thinly veiled tolerance, or outright exasperation is not lost on students' watchful eyes. Sadly, some students perceive that as a license to tease, demean, ostracize, or bully any classmate who displays an eccentricity of any kind.

In a community-centered classroom, the support and acceptance of peers for one another is significant and can contribute to the teacher's efforts to develop a positive relationship with a resistant learner. In a student-centered classroom led by a caring teacher, school becomes a happy "home away from home." For some students, such a positive atmosphere makes school an oasis in the desert.

RESILIENT RESISTERS

Resilience is the capacity to overcome adversity. It is another factor to consider when attempting to reach a resistant learner. This book has demonstrated that the possible causes of resistance and/or the motives behind resisting learning are varied and complex:

- Students who experience poor attachment with their primary caregivers are the most resistant to forming relationships with teachers or peers.
- Students who resist learning are quickly labeled failures, or worse.
- For students whose social and emotional growth and development are confined by antisocial behavior, nothing is more important than experiencing positive relationships.
- Students whose life experiences have been primarily negative have self-talk reinforced by feelings of self-hatred, incompetence, mistrust, and unhappiness.
- Resistant students are more vulnerable and more receptive to change in times of conflict when teachers guide them to see conflict as an opportunity for growth.
- Aggression is learned behavior that can be minimized by protecting students' safety, security, and self-image in school.
- Punishing noncompliant or uncooperative students fails to support motivation systems for learning.

Scores of daily in-class behaviors stem from these factors. They test every teacher's resolve to find ways to create a positive personal connection that might ultimately allow successful teaching and learning to occur. Resistant behavior demands so much attention that it is easy to overlook something about resistant students that could be singularly helpful. *Many resistant students are actively surviving against incredible odds.* Their efforts to survive force them to be resilient beyond any measure.

Like their peers, these students are creating an identity. Unlike many of their peers, each day's unpredictability hurriedly forces their growth and development forward, with little or no regard for typical age-appropriate milestones.

Outside of school, some students are completely responsible for the care and feeding of their siblings. Others care for parents addicted to drugs or alcohol; some try to protect themselves and their family from abusive or violent neighbors or neighborhood events. They learn to take advantage of whatever resources are available. They problem-solve. They display false bravado to engage in risky, negative, and dangerous adult activities that have implications that their incompletely developed brains cannot grasp.

Twenty years later, Mrs. Griffin still wonders whatever happened to A. J. Clear in her mind are the six months they spent together while she was his teacher and he was on long-term suspension from school. She regrets that she never really taught him much; A. J. was not disposed to learn at all. It surprised her that he showed up for class day after day because he rarely tried to work. When he did, he was surprisingly successful. He began to hang around her room during her free period before lunch. After lunch he was usually AWOL. Then and now, Mrs. Griffin thinks of A. J. as someone sent to teach her.

A. J.'s school records revealed a long, sad litany of school failure, troublesome behavior, and violent outbursts. His suspension referral stated, "Threat of harm to staff and endangering students by throwing a desk." A. J. craved attention. Most of his stories about his family were laced with loss, violence, neglect, and poverty. Mrs. Griffin's willingness to listen and interact without judgment showed a side of A. J. that few people knew. He was funny, insightful, kind, and much sadder than angry.

A most compelling story told of A. J.'s overnight experience alone in a drug house, left there by adults who knew a police raid would not matter much if a fourteen-year-old was the only one there. They told him he was their most responsible young seller. He recalled having an automatic weapon by his side but still being scared because he was uncertain how to use it and undecided whether he would try. He described a kitchen stocked with all a growing boy could want and luxurious chairs and big-screen TVs.

When anyone came to pay for drugs with food stamps, A. J. proudly told how he refused to sell to them, telling them to go feed their kids instead. Coins were thrown into a five-gallon bucket. He loved Saturday mornings, because the "bosses" allowed him and his buddies to go out into the street, yell "Money from heaven!," and toss the coins in the air while the neighborhood kids scrambled to get them.

As soon as they can, teachers should try to learn what life outside of school is like for the resistant students they hope to help. To recognize responsibility, caring, protectiveness, resourcefulness, creative problem solving, bravery, and kindness in the context of students' out-of-school life is to have a ready-made advantage toward building a positive relationship with them. Although those qualities in A. J. were undeniably and urgently in need of redirection, their presence was real and full of potential.

Known for his research on childhood resilience and his therapeutic work with children and families in the treatment of at-risk youth, Michael Ungar writes:

> Until we better understand children's strategies for resilience we will mistake our children's efforts for survival to be signs of dangerous, delinquent, deviant or disordered behavior. Children have shown me that problematic behaviors are still a search for health. These youth tell me that despite appearances to the contrary, they are all waking up each morning committed to surviving. [1]

Adults who manage to overcome adversity during their young years of growth and development universally identify one or more persons who were there to support them along the way. Frequently, that one person is a teacher. To be that teacher is one of the greatest and most profound rewards of the profession.

RESISTANCE VS. CULTURE CLASH

Sometimes, resistance to learning is not that at all. Students may need adaptation skills beyond their ability if their cultural background and life experience are different from or even opposite what is accepted and expected in their school district. *"Resisting" students may well be struggling to preserve the identity they have and want to keep, even if it means having a school persona that lives up to low expectations.*

African American students, Asian American students, Native American students, Mexican American students, and many other culturally diverse groups who choose to maintain and live by their traditions and customs have all encountered discrimination, prejudice, and stereotypical judgments based on the ignorant belief that white, middle-class students are superior learners overall.[2]

Membership and experiences in one or more groups that represent human diversity deeply affect student learning. Ethnicity, race, gender, religion, language, age, sexual orientation, ability, disability—each of these groups has shared beliefs, attitudes, values, goals, and practices that are distinctive. Members in each of these groups have been the targeted recipients of unequal treatment. Recall that the nature of students' and teachers experiences within these groups generates their self-talk. Whatever the self-talk is, it quickly connects to feelings that can lead to hasty actions—right or wrong.

Successful teaching requires recognizing the preconceived notions *students* may bring to school based on their membership in any given group that receives unequal treatment. *Teachers'* ability to set their own preconceived notions aside will help them make respect for *all students* a personal goal and a classroom rule. Personal interaction with the families and communities that represent these groups makes this challenge much easier.

Finding a way to build a positive personal connection that might lead to an influential relationship means teachers should seek out and welcome any opportunity to step out of their comfort zone to do it.

Mrs. Mandell: *"Hello, Mrs. Simpson. Is this a good time for me to call? I am Adriano's English teacher. I am calling to ask your advice. I know that you know Adriano much better than I ever will. I want to help him improve his English grade. Would you allow me to visit your home so we could talk together? I know your younger children keep you very busy there. I will be so grateful for your help. I could come any time after school. May I bring a treat for the children?"*

Mr. Brogan: *"Katya, my neighbor is Polish. I told her how happy I am to have you as my student this year, and she said your families go to the same church. Then she told me you and her son will be dancers at the Polish Festival in the spring. Tell me about that. I'd like to bring my family to the festival. I do know that some very delicious homemade food is there."*

Teachers whose actions take them beyond their comfort zone usually discover that the good that comes from doing so outweighs the effort. Their demonstrated openness and acceptance of differences is well received, especially because it is unexpected. Often, vital information about the families and communities from which students come sheds light on academic or behavioral issues at school. Person-to-person connections foster mutual understanding.

Legal permanent residents numbered 1.1 million in the United States in 2011. An estimated 11.5 million unauthorized immigrants live, work, and study in the United States. Hundreds of countries are represented in these numbers; Mexico, China, and India were the lead countries of birth, according to the Homeland Security Annual Flow Report for April 2012. Students from diverse cultures are typically present in school districts in every state. Beginning and veteran teachers alike find that their ability to teach effectively across cultures offers both taxing challenges and delightful opportunities.

The education profession calls teachers to develop awareness of, sensitivity to, competent knowledge about, and genuine appreciation of differences between and among students. Arriving at such a high degree of self-awareness does not come automatically at the completion of a teacher education program, or a seminar, or a particular course of study. It takes personal commitment, self-study, and consistent reflection. It takes observing others' actions and owning painful mistakes.

The "mistakes" in the following examples are not nearly as important as recognizing them and using them as opportunities for professional growth:

Example #1

Names are meant to be a source of empowerment and pride in every culture. In some cultures, names have great weight; they are selected for their meaning and meant to be portents of things to come. Yoichiro Ajibana's first day in history class began this way:

Mrs. Moira: *"Welcome, class! I hope we will have a good year together. Please say 'Present' when I call your name. John Davis . . . Steven Cramer . . . Darla Haywood . . . Sara Pinello . . . Um . . . Hmm* (audible inhaling, looking at Yoichiro) *I'm sorry, young man—say your name, please."*

"Yoichiro Ajibana."

"What? Could you say it again?"

"Yoichiro Ajibana."

"OK. My goodness. Do you have a nickname?"

Example #2

Nguyen Tan Dinh's father came to the United States first and worked as a researcher, saving his money until he could afford to bring his family here. During his second year, he actually won a significant lottery prize. When his son arrived, he was proud to enroll him in a private school. Dinh's transition to life in America and a new education system was difficult at best.

Ms. Travis, exasperated: *"Dinh, we are talking about your failing English grade. You are looking everywhere but at me. Are you listening? Look at me. I am explaining something very important to you."*

Ms. Travis did not know that in Vietnamese culture, corrections require downcast eyes, especially young to old, male to female. Yet, Dinh was in her class for two months before the conversation took place. Summaries of gestures, protocols, customs, and habits are readily available in books and online for anyone who wishes to learn basic information about interacting with a person from another country and culture. Ms. Travis should have known. After their exchange, Dinh knew only that his teacher is from a world very different from his own.

Example #3

Mr. Rose enjoyed a long-standing reputation as a counselor who tried to help students in any way he could. Joanne asked him if he could help her brother. Now seventeen, Keith was expressing interest in returning to school; he had not been since seventh grade. At that time, he had announced to his middle-school classmates that he was gay and began coming to school dressed as ostentatiously as possible. The stir caused by this led to his desired attention, but also trouble of all kinds. Eventually, Keith was suspended from school, and ultimately he dropped out. Mr. Rose agreed to meet with him after school. They agreed upon a plan for continuing his education.

Unfortunately, the stir caused by Keith's meeting with Mr. Rose rivaled the ones he had caused at the middle school years ago. Only this time, several teachers' conversations in the faculty room showed how first thoughts quickly overtake second thoughts that should prevail among professionals.

"Mercy! Did you see that kid who came to meet with Ron? Where did he come from?"

"He's Joanne's brother. Used to be here years ago. Got suspended. Looks about the same—on the nowhere train."

"I mean, come on . . . they aren't going to let him in high school. Imagine having him or her—whatever—in your class."

"That family's been a mess since forever. Look at Joanne."

"My detention kids ran to the door when he walked by. I just smiled and shook my head. Didn't say a word, though."

"Is that the same family where the dad just went to jail?"

"Joanne's dad is in jail? For what?"

Inadvertent offenses, stereotypical responses, damaging judgments, and statements that lack discretion occur. It is always regrettable, always a reminder of everyone's human imperfection. Most teachers are committed to continuous personal growth and devote an inordinate number of overtime hours to their profession. Nonetheless, the standard is high, and mistakes are far-reaching and long-lived.

Students are cheated out of their right to discuss differences and examine their own biases when they have teachers who lack self-awareness. Teachers sensitive to prejudice will not allow students to miss the opportunity to know and accept their classmates as individuals. Demanding teachers will expect and encourage all students to achieve academic excellence, making no assumptions based on race, ethnicity, or anything else. Joyful teachers will sincerely celebrate differences and honor them beyond a week, a month, or a chance to try chopsticks.

RECIPE FOR RELATING TO A RESISTANT STUDENT

The responsibility to address the needs of resistant students falls upon all teachers. A moral obligation requires teachers to attend to those who present themselves as unresponsive, marginalized, or impaired. More than their peers who are self-secure and self-reliant, resistant students depend upon teachers' capacity to help and compassion to care.

- *Make a conscious decision to consistently devote some time to engage with the student who is resisting learning,* whether or not you know why he is doing so. Be clear about your intention. Some examples might be addressing absenteeism, failure, bad behavior, worrisome withdrawal, sleeping in class, or offering simple kindness to someone in need. Always keep in mind that abandoning a budding relationship with a resistant student only reinforces his perception of adults as unreliable and insincere. Availability and consistent support are essential.
- *Reach out to the student.* Plan a personal exchange that invites the student to talk about himself. It can be a brief exchange or a longer meeting. Make "small talk." Set the student at ease. Smile often. Ask about favorite pets, sports, TV shows, candy bars, or colors. React to answers. Keep notes. Be sincere in saying you are glad to get to know the student a little bit. Share something about yourself with the student. In conversation, use an adult-person-to-young-person affect, rather than teacher-in-authority-to-obedient-student tone. Remember at least one favorite item for later reference. Do not address sensitive classroom issues at this first personal communication attempt.
- *Find a reason to say something personal every day* after the initial attempt to connect. Mention a favorite if possible to show that something said was important to remember. Maybe bring a favorite color folder or candy bar or sports magazine. Offer it spontaneously—never as a bribe.
- *Respond differently from the student's expectations if he tests you.* During class interactions, remember to avoid unnecessary power struggles, punishment, and bribes of any kind. Every time you react differently from what a student expects, you force him to question the self-talk that underpins his negative beliefs.
- *Arrange another meeting if your goal is to get the student to change his behavior.* Remember that deciding to make a change in personal behavior begins a process that takes time. It takes experiencing many acts of kindness, for example, to offset the experience of one act of unkindness.
- *Use I-messages to state your concern as simply as possible.* For example, *"I feel . . . when you . . ."* or *"I cannot teach when . . . and this makes me feel . . ."* or *"I need your help to solve this problem."* I-messages are not

accusatory. They rightly identify the problem as something owned by both parties, setting the stage for a cooperative solution. Students rarely realize that what they do affects their teacher personally.

- *Suggest all the reasons you can think of that might account for the issue you wish to address. "I'm wondering if . . ."* or *"I'm thinking that . . ."* or *"Maybe this is what is happening. Am I right?"* Students have great difficulty in expressing the reasons or motives for what they do because true introspection requires a high degree of cognitive competence and insightful vocabulary. By offering possibilities, the student can agree or disagree more easily. In either case, you will be able to lead him to problem-solve with you.

- *Transfer the ownership of the problem to the student*, assuring him of your genuine support and practical help. Ask, *"How can we solve this problem? I can promise you I will be as helpful as I can be."* Write down an agreed-upon solution. Sign it together. Look for even the smallest attempt to change, and show the student you have noticed it. Do not be overly effusive—only sincere.

- Mutually schedule another meeting. At it, *congratulate the student on progress. If there has been none, point out the consequences that his choices have had.* For example, lost privileges, negative phone calls home, continued poor grades, troubles in the cafeteria. Emphasize that the student truly has control over negative outcomes, and problem-solve again. Assure the student that you understand change is difficult. Help the student see that who we are is different from what we do—that you don't "like" him any less for making mistakes. Offer no bribes as an added incentive to try harder.

- *Follow this meeting as soon as possible with some kind of spontaneous positive reinforcement.* By now, the student will begin to see you in a new light and think of you as a caring teacher who may deserve trust. If the student begins to believe he is capable of change, you have earned a bonus. If he actually begins to change, you have won the lottery.

- *Continue to support the student no matter what happens.* Your own growth, transformation even, may surprise you. By interacting with one, ideas for interacting with others will come. By helping one, you will see more clearly the potential of all.

But what if this recipe fails? Despite all efforts, what if no positive personal connection occurs? Time and reflection will put a failed attempt to build a relationship with a resistant student in perspective. Most relevant is remembering that only the person who owns a particular behavior or attitude can change it. To connect with every student is an impossible expectation. Rejection is an inherent risk in every relationship.

Teachers plant seeds; they cannot know if all of them grow. What appears to be a failure may not be a failure at all. Many adults, many years later, can quote verbatim admonitions and advice from teachers.

Teacher. By virtue of that title alone, teachers have power. They can influence students. Daily occurrences make many teachers pause, rightly humbled that small deeds carry such great weight. Spontaneous rewards of all kinds, insignificant by themselves, make so many students truly happy. Notes from a teacher appear years later, carefully saved in someone's memory box. Merit certificates remain on the refrigerator door until yellowed with age. School stories are handed down from one generation to the next.

The greatest privilege afforded by the power given to teachers is to touch young lives, to help make a difference in the way they see themselves and their place in the world. This vision celebrates the ideal outcome of every student's education. However, human teachers and human students are in schools, and the ideal goal is plagued by the imperfections of both.

Teachers' power allows them to create rules; select curricular content; choose topics and discussions; deliver rewards, punishments, judgments, inferences, and even assign motives. Teachers' actions and students' reactions make the education experience mostly positive or mostly negative at the end of the journey.

As adults in authority, the power teachers have over students is formidable. The role of giver is assigned to teachers automatically, implying that those who receive are lucky winners. Sadly missing from this assumption is the role that students play as teachers of their teachers. This book suggests that making positive personal connections with students and building relationships will enrich the teacher as much as they enrich the student.

When teachers enter the real world of students and their families and come to know them through insight and experience, something happens. Commonalities overshadow differences. Students' and teachers' attitudes change, as does their mutual appreciation. Trust increases. It becomes possible and likely that teachers will reach students as well as teach them.

POINTS TO REMEMBER

- Behavior management evolves from cooperation and participation; discipline is rooted in accepting responsibility for free choices.
- Many resistant students are actively surviving against incredible odds. Learning about and considering students' life outside of school greatly increases teachers' efforts to help.
- Membership and experiences in one or more groups that represent human diversity deeply affect student learning. Every group has shared beliefs,

attitudes, values, goals, and practices that are distinctive but often targets them for unequal treatment.
- Teachers who resolve to attend to students who are unresponsive, marginalized, or impaired rarely regret doing so.

NOTES

1. Ungar, Michael. *Nurturing Hidden Resilience in Troubled Youth.* Toronto, Ontario, Canada: University of Toronto Press, Scholarly Publishing Division, 2004.

2. Delpit, Lisa. *Other People's Children.* New York: The New Press, 1995.

References

Bandura, Albert. *Social Foundations of Thought and Action.* Upper Saddle River, NJ: Prentice Hall, 1986.

Brendtro, Larry K., Martin Brokenleg, and Steve VanBockern. *Reclaiming Youth at Risk: Our Hope for the Future.* Bloomington, IN: National Educational Service, 1990.

Cloud/Springfield, John. "Of Arms and the Boy," *Time*, June 2001, 38.

Deci, Edward L., and Richard Flaste. *Why We Do What We Do.* New York: Penguin Books, 1996.

Delpit, Lisa. *Other People's Children.* New York: The New Press, 1995.

Erikson, E. H. *Childhood in Society.* P. 17 in *Educational Psychology*, by Anita Woolfolk. Upper Saddle River, NJ: Pearson Education, Inc., 2010.

Gardner, Howard. *Frames of Mind.* New York: Basic Books, 2011.

———. "A Multiplicity of Intelligences." *Scientific American*, Winter 1998.

Goldstein, Arnold, and Barry Glick. *Aggression Replacement Training.* Champaign, IL: Research Press, 1987.

Goleman, Daniel. *Working with Emotional Intelligence.* New York: Bantam Doubleday Dell Publishing Group, 1998.

Jung, Carl G. *Psychological Types.* Princeton, NJ: Princeton University Press, 1921.

Kohl, Herbert. *I Won't Learn from You.* New York: The New Press, 1995.

Kohn, Alfie. *Punished by Rewards.* New York: Houghton Mifflin Company, 1993.

Long, Nicholas J., and William C. Morse. *Conflict in the Classroom.* Austin, TX: Pro-Ed, 1996.

Maeroff, Gene I. *Altered Destinies: Making Life Better for Children in Need.* New York: Palgrave Macmillan, 1999.

Magid, Ken, and Carole A. McKelvey. *High Risk: Children without a Conscience.* Golden, CO: M & M Publishing, 1987.

McClelland, David C. *Human Motivation.* Cambridge, UK: Cambridge University Press, 2000.

Noddings, Nell. *The Challenge to Care in Schools.* New York: Teachers College Press, 1992.

Purkey, William Watson. *What Students Say to Themselves.* Thousand Oaks, CA: Corwin Press, 2000.

Silver, Harvey F., and Richard W. Strong. *Learning Styles and Strategies.* Trenton, NJ: Thoughtful Education Press, 1996.

Silver, Harvey F., Richard W. Strong, and Matthew J. Perini. *So Each May Learn.* Alexandria, VA: Association for Supervision and Curriculum Development, 2000.

Skinner, B. F. *Beyond Freedom and Dignity.* New York: Alfred A. Knopf, 1971.

Sokolov, A. N. *Inner Speech and Thought.* New York: Plenum, 1972.

Ungar, Michael. *Nurturing Hidden Resilience in Troubled Youth.* Toronto, Ontario, CAN: University of Toronto Press, Scholarly Publishing Division, 2004.

Vygotsky, L. S. *The Genetic Roots of Thinking and Speech.* P. 45 in *Educational Psychology*, by Anita Woolfolk. Upper Saddle River, NJ: Pearson Education, Inc., 2010.

Woolfolk, Anita. *Educational Psychology.* Upper Saddle River, NJ: Pearson Education Ltd., 2010.

About the Author

Mary Skvorak and her husband live in Walworth, New York, where open fields and woods around their home offer the opportunity to enjoy a variety of wildlife and birds that come to visit. Mary is retired now, except for teaching an occasional course at Nazareth College of Rochester. Her experiences as an administrator, college instructor, teacher, mentor, staff developer, international education facilitator, and consultant for her business, Behavior Management Applications, enabled her to write this book about building relationships with students with enthusiasm and conviction. She considers education to be the profession that exceeds all others in its importance because of its profound influence on the lives of learners of all ages. Their success in turn, truly determines the outcome of world events and the future of the planet.

Having more time to be with family, to visit a son in Ohio, to actually weed the garden and can some vegetables, to read, to write, and to enjoy music by personal choice are wonderful gifts. When considering retirement after nearly five decades in the education field, Mary hoped to make the words on a ceramic plaque in the kitchen apply to her life more authentically. It reads: A little more laughter, a little less worry, a little more kindness, a little less hurry. *That* is still a work in progress!